The SHROPSHIRE Cook Book

A celebration of the amazing food & drink on our doorstep.
Featuring over 35 stunning recipes.

The Shropshire Cook Book

©2017 Meze Publishing. All rights reserved.

First edition printed in 2017 in the UK.

ISBN: 978-1-910863-32-9

Thank you to: Chris Burt
Beth Heath, Shropshire Festivals

Compiled by: Anna Tebble

Written by: Aaron Jackson

Photography by:
Tim Green (www.timgreenphotographer.co.uk)
Paul Carroll (www.paulcarrollphoto.com)

Edited by: Phil Turner

Designed by: Matt Crowder, Paul Cocker,
Jake Cowlishaw

PR: Kerre Chen

Cover art: Luke Prest (www.lukeprest.com)

Contributors: Sarah Koriba, Laura Wolvers

me:ze
PUBLISHING

Published by Meze Publishing Limited
Unit 1b Rialto
2 Kelham Square
Kelham Riverside
Sheffield S3 8SD
Web: www.mezepublishing.co.uk
Tel: 0114 275 7709
Email: info@mezepublishing.co.uk

Printed by Bell & Bain Ltd, Glasgow

FOREWORD

Shropshire chef Chris Burt explains what it is about Shropshire that keeps him coming back for more...

The modern chef is a curious beast. We still make our bread and butter in the kitchen, sometimes literally. But while one eye is on the incoming tickets, the other has to be on the bigger picture. We're as adept at surfing the surging waves of social media as we are sourcing the best of local produce. We are, to coin a twenty-first century phrase, glocal. This is why you find me writing this foreword while packing for another food adventure. After all, the chef who can't effortlessly multi-task isn't a chef.

I find nowadays that travel makes me cranky as well as efficient – again, a state that every chef recognizes. I suppose it's because I'm leaving Shropshire, my home. It reminds me that I've always been travelling, even when maybe I didn't know it.

My own journey started in fairly humble beginnings in Yorkshire. I left to earn my stripes as a chef in the Big Smoke of London, as many chefs have before me and many will in future. But the move to Shropshire took me by surprise. It was an unexpected jink in the journey. It was the old, old story, of course. Boy meets girl, boy moves to Shropshire. I didn't see it coming, but this boy has been here ever since.

And with good reason too. What's in Shropshire is in this book that you're holding. It's the heart of England, a landscape crammed to bursting with some of the finest produce that this scepter'd isle can bring into being. It's home to adventurous chefs, royal-standard restaurants, eclectic eateries, and markets crammed with the fat of the land and the fruit of the loom. It's a county whose untouched hedgerows, rolling hills, and temperate climate and warm, welcoming, friendly people have inspired poets. It's a place where everything good about traditional ways and values are there for those who want them, but so too is everything that's best and brightest about contemporary Britain and British food.

So while I'm excited to be off again in search of adventure, it doesn't take me long to remember that the best bit about going away is that you get to come home again. Home to Shropshire; to warm welcomes, loving arms, good food, and the best company.

Not even jet-lag can touch that feeling.

Chris Burt

Chef proprietor at The Peach Tree, Momo No Ki and Havana Republic

CONTENTS

Time to CELEBRATE!

In Shropshire, festivals aren't lifestyle choices. They're ways of life, and celebrations of living...

A festival means different things to different people. For the young, it might be a rite-of-passage experience, a way of coming together with friends or a small gesture of independence on the journey to adulthood. For adults, bogged down in the workaday round of raising children and paying bills it might mean a chance to slough off those cares for a while and let down what's left of their hair. Ask anyone and they'll give you a different definition of why they love them. Some will say it's about the music, or the vibe, or the people, or the chance to sleep in six inches of mud in a collapsing tent with a three-hour wait for a toilet. Different strokes, as they say, for different folks.

In Shropshire, though, festivals aren't part of a millennial trend. They do them differently, for a start. They're simultaneously part of Shropshire's history and its story in the present. In Shropshire, they're a way of life and always have been. You see, Britain's history is stitched into it's landscapes. From Hadrian marking the outer limits of the known world with his wall across the North of this country to the cairns and standing stones of Scotland's wilds down to the contours of the Kent coast and beyond, there isn't a part of this land of ours that doesn't have a story to tell about its people and their ways since time immemorial. In Shropshire's case it's a story of England. This, after all, is the county of Housman's 'blue remembered hills'; of the lads that would never grow old; and the powerful nostalgia that comes from remembering a beloved homeland. This is the England of the green and pleasant land, of pleasant people, long summers and rural idyll. This is England as we remember it even if we've spent our lives living in the big city. It's also an England where coming together to celebrate all that's good is a way of life.

In Shropshire, they've never forgotten that, which is why they've been hosting festivals here since time out of mind – which is probably why they do them so well. Shropshire's calendar is studded with festivals both big and small. Take a closer look at them, though, and you'll find a significant number of them have Beth Heath and her company Shropshire festivals helping to organise and pull them together. Take the Shrewsbury Food Festival – a good example considering the subject matter of this book. Fired into life by a couple of friends eager to celebrate Shropshire's abundance of fantastic produce it's grown to be one of Shropshire's biggest events of the year.

SYTCH FARM STUDIOS

Hand thrown stoneware pottery
Handmade English hardwood boards
Made in Shropshire

01743 718908
sytchfarmstudios.com

It's not just a celebration of the fantastic bounty that can be drawn from Shropshire's iconic, unforgettable countryside. It's also a celebration of the fact that some of the best chefs and food producers in the country work in the county; a celebration of good food and the fact that good food is best enjoyed in good company and convivial surroundings. It's a formula that works too. This event alone draws crowds of over 26,000, keen to sample not only the great food on display (with many of the contributors to this book displaying their wares at it), but the friendly atmosphere and multitude of events and activities. Both Ludlow and Shrewsbury might also be vying (in a friendly way) for the title of Shropshire's food Mecca but the competition means that the overall result is manna from heaven for foodies everywhere.

Nor is it simply the food that makes Shropshire such a great place to visit. There's countryside built for walking through and history writ large in every landscape, whether urban or rural. Oh, and did we mention the festivals? There's the Shrewsbury Folk Festival, one of the UK's biggest and best, attracting the luminaries of the scene and the up-and-coming artists to watch. For those with their diaries out, there's also the Shropshire Kids Festival, Shropshire County Show, Shropshire Oktoberfest and Shrewsbury's Christmas celebrations. In each instance, the emphasis is about providing a memorable experience. Anyone who has ever been to a

badly-run festival knows just how much an over-long queue for the toilets and just too many people milling around can put a crimp in even the most amiable soul. But Shropshire Festivals, and the events that they organise, focus on the quality of the attendee experience throughout, rather than on cramming as many people onsite as possible and hoping for the best. Looking at the history of the county – which is one of warm welcomes and fulsome hospitality – it would be easy to surmise that the former rather than the latter is the Shropshire way. There's a wealth of experience that goes into each one. Beth has a proven track record in the area alongside an excellent record as an entrepreneur and businesswoman.

So, when you visit Shropshire you will find all of the things that wrote it into the narrative of the nation. The untouched hedgerows, rolling hills and temperate climate are still there. But this isn't some Edwardian fantasy, a backwater, a land that time forgot. This is a living, breathing county, with a warm and friendly welcome for visitors and a host of things to do and see. To find out more about the amazing festivals in Shropshire go to www.shropshirefestivals.co.uk and the full lineup of events in Shrewsbury www.originalshrewsbury.co.uk

Oh, and did we mention that the food is fantastic? Well, just turn the pages of this book to find out for yourself...

A slice of HISTORY

With its wonderfully storied past, Albright Hussey Manor Hotel balances the best of old and new in one of England's most beautiful regions.

When it comes to evocative histories, Albright Hussey's is illustrious. Recorded in William the Conqueror's Domesday Book it has endured and experienced a millennium of British history. But the family-owned and managed award-winning hotel and restaurant now offers a shining contemporary testament to what can be achieved in the present with vision, artistry, hard work and high standards.

Under the stewardship of owner Paul Subbiani, as a hotel Albright Hussey makes the most of its period charm to offer an appealing site for those simply looking to get away from it all for a break or those wanting a venue for a special or celebratory occasion. Individually designed and appointed, each of the 26 has its own unique character, blending the appeal of the Grade-II listed Tudor building with modern amenities.

Holding two AA rosettes, the kitchen and restaurant have consistently achieved and maintained similarly high standards. The oak-panelling, original beams, huge open fireplace of the Moat Room are perfectly complemented by food prepared by Albright Hussey's chef Michel Nijsten and his team. The evening, lunch, gourmet, private dining and afternoon tea menus are all underpinned by an admirable ethos. Michel visits Shropshire's producers, some of the finest in Britain, to make sure that quality and consistency remains of the very highest standard from the fields to the plate. Much is made of the idea of 'local produce' nowadays, but it's quite another thing to be able to look out of the window as a chef and see the beef that your establishment uses in the nearby fields as Michel can. The quality available in the county is possibly why after an illustrious career trajectory that has taken in the Hosteellerie de Hamert and the Savoy and Hilton Park Lane in London, Michel has settled and remained in Shropshire at the Albright Hussey, building its formidable reputation for providing wonderful dining experiences.

From the simple Smoked and Cured Salmon with Lime and Horse Radish on the Evening Menu to the rich Medallion of Beef Fillet with Oxtail on the Gourmet Menu, across the board the emphasis, as you might expect, is on letting the ingredients shine in sympathetic and inspired flavour combinations. As the recipes contained in this section indicate, Albright Hussey works very closely with the best local suppliers to provide unforgettable taste, dining, and residential experiences for all of its guests.

Bennett & Dunn
SALSA DRESSING

We're spoilt for choice when it comes to culinary oil, but one of the very best is Bennett and Dunn cold pressed rapeseed oil. Run by the husband and wife team of Rupert and Tracey Bennett, the company produces cold-pressed, triple-filtered, hand-bottled rapeseed oil drawn from Shropshire's irresistible landscape. Rupert and Tracey started the company in 2014 after watching celebrity chefs on the television cooking with, and recommending cold pressed rapeseed oil as a British alternative to extra virgin olive oil. Rupert has a farming background and Tracey has years of experience in retail. The couple quickly found that the product they were producing was of a high quality, this is due in part to Rupert's dedication to quality, he keeps a tea spoon next to the press and tastes the oil at least once a day to make sure that it is always perfect. Harvested in late July the seeds are cleaned and then stored ready to be pressed to order every month, ensuring the oil is always as fresh as possible when bottled. The oil is extracted by gently squeezing the seed, a traditional process that keeps the flavour, texture and health benefits of the oil intact. It is triple-filtered and bottled by hand. Nothing is added between the fields and the bottle so the result is a deliciously flavoured oil, whose creamy nutty flavour makes it ideal for dipping and drizzling, as well as for dressings and Marinades. Cold pressed rapeseed oil also has the highest burn point of any culinary oil, which makes it perfect to use from roasts to stir-fries too. Cold pressed Rapeseed oil has many health benefits, it contains half the saturated fat of olive oil, it also has the lowest saturated fat content of any culinary oil, it is rich in Omega 3 and 6 which is proven to lower cholesterol as part of a good diet. Their oil is dairy free GM free, gluten-free and is suitable for vegetarians. The winner of a Great Taste Award it's little surprise that this home-grown wonder has become the oil of choice for many of Shropshire's and the UK`s finest restaurants, including Albright Hussey Manor Hotel and Aqua Shard in London. Bennett & Dunn oils are also available to buy at many quality delis, farm shops and independent retailers in Shropshire and across the UK.

Preparation time: 10 minutes

Ingredients

2 red onions

2 green peppers

2 green chillies

1 clove garlic

2 tbsp rape seed oil

2 limes, juiced

8 tomatoes concasse (crushed or ground)

Salt

Method

Dicing the red onion, peppers chillies and garlic, add the salt, juice of 2 limes, and oil in a suitable bowl. Then, fold in the diced concasse tomatoes and season to taste. This is a perfect dressing to accompany a summery salad, especially any including an avocado pear or freshly grilled tuna steak.

Liquid HISTORY

Deep in the heart of Shropshire, Tanner's Wine Merchants has been providing our drops of the good stuff for nearly two centuries now...including supplying the Albright Hussey Manor Patrons for half a century.

We are addicted to the new nowadays. Barely before we've got our latest smartphone out of the box, and long before we've actually worked out how to use it properly, we're hankering after the next model. The latest thing, the newest fad, the next big thing – we've been conditioned to think that these are the things that tick our boxes. But when you really think about it, you can't beat something that's stood the test of time. You can't argue with something that's endured the vagaries of history and isn't just still standing, but is actually thriving in the here and now.

Take Tanner's Wine Merchants. Queen Victoria had barely been on the throne for two years when Shropshire lad William Tanner went to sea. She still had sixty years to reign when he returned from travelling far foreign lands, took his brother H. Edward into partnership and founded W & H. E Tanner, wine merchants, in Shrewsbury in 1842. 175 years later, Tanner's is still here. It's still family-run, by the fourth generation of the Tanner family to take the reins no less. And it's still Britain's pre-eminent independent wine-merchant. Tanner's has a string of industry awards and accolades to its name acknowledging this. But nice though it is to have it, the critical acclaim springs from a commitment to quality, service and value that's as evident today as it was when William Tanner returned from his voyages and first launched the business. Take a simple thing. The company has expanded over the years. Tanners now has seven outlets and employs 100 people, largely split between its Welsh distribution centre and its headquarters in Shrewsbury. 12 of them have been with the company for more than 30 years. You can't buy that sort of loyalty – and you certainly can't buy the sort of service and reputation that can only be built by a core of long-serving staff.

Tanner's service and reputation are traditional in the best sense of the word. It's backed up by the sort of knowledge that only comes from being in the business for nearly two centuries. It's the sort of knowledge that comes from having imported, sourced, and sold everything from wine to butts of sherry; from bottled beer to mineral water; from claret and burgundy from France to rum from Jamaica and Guyana to whisky from Ireland and Scotland over a staggering period of time, but one crucially connected by the family who have steered the business through the choppy waters of history throughout. It's a name synonymous with quality, which is why Shropshire, England, Britain, and some of the world's highest-quality restaurants, hotels, and outlets turn to Tanners when it comes to compiling their wine list.

Tanners Wines

 Lane Cottage
Produce

"100% Good for you,
grown naturally, nothing artificial"

Wash before use
Keep refrigerated
4-6°c

01568 770720
www.lanecottageproduce.co.uk

Grown
Here fordshire

Lane Cottage Produce
SALADETTE OF SHREWSBURY FRESH CHEESE

As with many of the best things in life, Lane Cottage Produce is what happens when preparation meets opportunity. Owners Richard and Amanda Sidgwick already had a lifetime of experience in agriculture and food when they moved to their small holding on the borders of Herefordshire and Shropshire. The hadn't been farmed for years – meaning that no artificial pesticides or fertilisers had been used on it. Their initial idea – to start a market garden selling more unusual varieties of leaves and crops – was so successful that demand for the good stuff they were growing outstripped supply. Lane Cottage Produce has established a reputation for quality and seasonality that means that it's the first choice for some of Shropshire's finest restaurants and foodie havens from the Ludlow Food Centre to Michel at Albright and Hussey to the likes of The Haughmond and beyond. The secret is the best natural foods and ingredients, naturally grown – organic fertilisers and sympathetic planting to keep pests away are the order of the day here. Wildlife abounds, and nothing artificial is used either in the polytunnels or the open fields. It's the traditional way and the result is a paean to Shropshire's landscape: fresh, seasonal produce that absolutely bursts with flavour!

Preparation time: 1 hour | Serves 4

Ingredients

100g mixed Lane Cottage fresh leaves

50g toasted pine nuts

100g purple potatoes, diced and cooked al dente

250g Mr Moyden's handmade Shrewsbury cheese

50ml Bennett & Dunn rapeseed oil

Fresh garden herbs, to taste

300g fresh crusty bread

½ lemon, juiced

Sea salt, to taste

Black pepper, freshly ground

Method

Cut the cheese into 16 equal portions before marinating for 1 hour in the oil, lemon juice and seasoning. Then, place the leaves in a large mixing bowl, and add the toasted pine nuts and diced potatoes. Draining the marinade from the cheese, toss half the juice over the leaves lightly before dividing between four salad bowls. Placing four slices of cheese on each, garnish with the fresh garden herbs, and serve with the crusty bread. Simple, but delicious!

Special Spuds
JALVING'S SPECIAL SPUD CRISPS AND FRIES

Have you ever wondered why artisan potato crisps command such a high price? They're just potatoes, right? With a little help from Jalving's Special Spuds Michel Nijsten shows you how to take the fight to the big boys by making your own, with a fries recipe thrown in for good measure!

Run by husband-and-wife team Gerrol and Alison Jalving, Jalving Potatoes are continually cross-breeding to develop and introduce potato varieties to give the humble but essential spud more flavour, colour and nutritional benefit. Our standard potato was anything but when it was first introduced to Europe from Peru in the sixteenth century. They were multi-coloured marvels with wonderfully shaped tubers. The potato we know today is the result of cross-breeding and selection to introduce uniformity and produce more tubers per plant. It's certainly worked, but perhaps at the cost of the inherent flavours and colours a potato is capable of, as well as its natural pest and disease resistance. Potatoes are naturally full of anti-oxidants and vitamins A, B1, B2, B3, C, and E. This bounty bumps up again when the flesh colours are more vibrant. Think yellows, purples and reds. Jalving potatoes are passionate about combining these original qualities with modern varieties. The result has been potatoes that produce lots of tubers, taste fantastic, and pack a nutritional punch. Oh, and they look absolutely fantastic too. Grown with minimal mechanical input and harvested by hand, it's been a slow process but already Jalving potatoes have become first choice at many local restaurants and are already a hit with the buying public. With potato-breeding being the family business (Gerrol's parents are still active in the field over in the Netherlands and the third generation is starting to get involved!) there's literally no limit to what can be achieved with the humble spud – a British staple, and in these hands a Shropshire speciality!

Preparation time: 10 minutes | Cooking time: 5 minutes | Serves 4

Ingredients

Choose any or all from the following four of Jalving's varieties: Royal Hussey Blue, Erika, Secret Severn, or Blushing Beauty

200g of any variety (for crisps); 400g (for chips)

15g salt

2l Bennett & Dunn rapeseed oil (for crisps or chips)

Method

To make crisps, wash and peel the potatoes before slicing them in a mandoline slicer into 1mm thick discs. Do not wash the potatoes after slicing! This washes away all of the flavour and goodness. Heat the oil to 145°c in a tall pan or a small fryer before carefully adding the discs. Try and retain the colour as you heat them. Overcooking will see them darken. They're done when they're crisp – the clue really is in the title!

To make fries, essentially follow the same process, heating the oil to the same temperature but cut the potatoes into 10mm x 10mm strips before frying gently. They're done when they start to gently float to the top.

Moydens Cheese
MOYDEN'S CHEESE FOUR WAYS

Since launching in 2005, Martin and Beth Moyden have established Moyden's Handmade Cheese as a highly-respected artisan cheesemakers, noted for their passion for quality, attention to detail and lust for perfection.

Inspired by his grandmother's tales of farming and food production, Martin was fascinated by the way in which a simple way of preserving milk with a history stretching back 9000 years was still being used today. The difference, of course, is that cheese-making happens on a mass-produced scale nowadays. The uniformity this promotes means that many of the recipes that tied distinctive cheese to different locations have been lost. Determined to emphasize these links, Martin began developing traditional cheese recipes that display a cheese's provenance.

From these beginnings, Moyden's has developed an ever-increasing range of cheeses, including Wrekin White, Wrekin Blue, Newport, Newport 1665, Caer Caradoc and Ironbridge Blue. The proof of a cheese is in the eating, and Moyden's cheeses do themselves proud in this regard, holding a number of local and national awards, including three golds at the British Cheese Awards.

Each has a story to tell. The Wrekin Blue, for example, is named after the Wrekin hill, a prominent and well-known landmark rising 1335 feet above the Shropshire Plain and featuring an Iron Age hill fort on the summit almost eight hectares in size. Newport 1665 commemorates the year of the Great Fire of Newport in 1665. It destroyed the homes of 166 families and caused £30,000 worth of damage (a huge sum in those days) – but rumour has it that it was an exceptional year for smoked cheese!

Now well-established and a trusted supplier to many of Shropshire's best restaurants and eateries, Moyden's Handmade Cheese's mission to keep artisan cheese-making and the heavenly flavours such processes promote alive and well is well and truly on track!

Preparation time: 10 minutes | Cooking time: 5 minutes | Serves 4

Ingredients

200g Wrekin Blue cheese shaped in balls

150g Smoked Newport

100g Caer Caradoc

100g Shrewsbury Fresh

4 x 50g Jerusalem artichokes

100ml milk

100g breadcrumbs,

1egg

Flour, a dusting

1 Gelatine leaf

Cayenne pepper, to taste

½ pint buttermilk

Method

To make the Newport panna cotta, melt the cheese with the milk in a pan, seasoning to taste. Add the gelatine and when it has dissolved pour into your preferred moulds. Leave to set and then turn out before serving.

To make the sorbet of Shrewsbury Fresh, warm the buttermilk and dissolve the cheese into it, seasoning to taste. Churn in a sorbetiere till smooth and set enough. Place in a freezer to set, and shape into quenelles 5 minutes before serving.

To make the Caer Caradoc crumble, wash the artichokes before peeling and drying. Hollow the artichoke and cook until tender. Then grate the cheese into the hollow centre, filling it. Meanwhile, make crumbs of the dried skin, mixed with a little grated cheese. Sprinkle over, and then at 175°c, 8 minutes before serving.

To make the Wrekin Blue, shape the cheese into balls. Beat the egg in a bowl and coat the balls in breadcrumbs by dipping first in flour, then in egg, and then in the breadcrumbs. Put to one side. These are to be deep-fried at 175°c, 3 minutes before serving.

Past and future PERFECT

Nestled among some of the best of Shropshire's green and pleasant land, there's something special going on down at Apley Farm Shop...

Tradition runs through the Apley Farm Shop. The sprawling estate it stands in can be traced back to an England before the restoration of the monarchy in the late-seventeenth century. Now owned and managed by the Hamilton family, the landscape represents a slice of Shropshire countryside so stunning that Queen Victoria considered Apley Hall as a country residence before P.G. Wodehouse reputedly drew on its charms to create the idyllic Blandings Castle, the home of the immortal Lord Emsworth and his prize pig, Empress. As Britain stood against a certain moustachioed dictator who, it is rumoured, had earmarked the Hall for his own residence, the estate served its country well, producing prize-winning cattle, milk, butter, and cheese, as well as potatoes, sugar beet and arable crops for the war effort.

Since its launch in 2011, however, Apley Farm Shop itself has recognized and exceeded the expectations and requirements of today's customers by establishing its own tradition of innovation and forward-thinking that acknowledges the estate's rich history even as it adds to it.

Apley Farm Shop's hub is the Shropshire Food Hall, a converted cattle shed amid whose high ceilings and elegant brickwork award-winning cheese was made in the past. Home now to the Creamery Café it offers a range of produce to gladden the hearts of the gourmand and the hearty diner alike. Local food from local producers for local people (and those who venture from further afield) is Apley's ethos and boy does it deliver the goods.

'The butchery counter was central to our original plans,' explains Lord Hamilton. 'We wanted to sell the estate's beef, venison and game when it was available.' But so too was drawing everything the estate has to offer under one roof. Coming back into production in 2013, Apley's 2-acre walled garden supplies picked seasonal fruits and vegetables to the chef at the café, local restaurants and the casual shopper alike. Similarly, the delicatessen offers pies and pastries made onsite, as well as a huge range of cheeses, cold meats, condiments and dressings.

Throw in the amenities of a thriving craft studio specialising in pottery and painting, a playbarn for children, a thriving plant centre and animal park and it's easy to see why Apley lives up to its motto. It does indeed offer the visitor so much more than a farm shop...

APLEY
WALLED GARDEN

A rich HISTORY

On the site of one of the bloodiest clashes in England's history, the battle for good food is being fought and won...

It's said that you're never far from history in Britain – a proverb as true in storied Shropshire as anywhere in the country. But at Battlefield 1403, you aren't just close to history. You're surrounded by it. This is the place where English archers first faced each other on English soil and the challenge of Northumbria's upstart Lord Henry Percy to Henry IV ended for good. You're aware of this, of course, as you walk around the site nowadays. If the 100-hectare battlefield and church erected over the pit where the dead protagonists were buried don't tip you the wink, well, the clue is in the title, after all. But history continues to be made here, in the form of Battlefield 1403's farm shop.

It's more than a farm shop, you see. It has one of the best butcheries in the UK attached to it, with beef and lamb sourced directly from the farm. Only launched in 2010, Battlefield's Delicatessen has already made the Independent's list of the 50 best delis in the UK, a testament to the quality on offer and an enduring reputation of selling the best locally produced cheeses and charcuterie – as well as the highest quality produce from further afield. Both provide the meats and cheeses used daily in Sparrow's café.

The above name was deliberately chosen to link the present generation to those who lived and worked to build Albrighton. They would recognize what their descendants are doing foodwise in showcasing the best local and seasonal produce on their menus – but with hearty classics like Battlefield beef and Shropshire Ale Pie always on offer. It's the sort of place where you can just as easily drop in for a fantastic Afternoon Tea as you can a filling lunch, or even book out for parties or business events.

Throw in that there's an exhibition detailing the rich historical events that have given the present business its name that vividly brings the past to life and a falconry centre where trained and experienced handlers can help you get close to some of the world's most beautiful raptors ... and well, it's easy to see why Battlefield 1403 is such a popular destination: great food, great service, and a great atmosphere with lots to do in a landscape that drips with rich history – all gathered in one place.

Battlefield 1403
SLOWLY BRAISED LAMB HENRY

This new and popular dish on Battlefield 1403's spring menu uses lamb henry from its butchery which in turn uses lamb sourced direct from the estate itself. One of Battlefield butchery's most popular cuts, this recipe uses the juices from the lamb throughout so that the flavour and the quality of the meat shines through.

Preparation time: 3.5 hours | Cooking time: 3-4 hours | Serves 4

Ingredients

4 lamb henry cuts (ask your butcher for these)

2 lamb bones, roasted

500ml red wine

Shallots, a bunch, chopped

Fresh rosemary, 1 sprig

500g baby or chantenay carrots

1 large leek

100g smoked bacon

2 white onions

1 kg waxy potatoes (such as Desiree)

100g butter, melted

Method

First, make the stock by roasting the lamb bones at 180°c (fan – 190°c conventional) for 30-35 minutes. Then, place the bones in a large pan, adding the wine, shallots, rosemary and enough water to cover the bones. Boil for around 3 hours, topping the water up as necessary to keep the bones covered.

Once the stock is ready, prepare the lamb and vegetables. Begin by sealing your lamb henry cuts in a pan over a medium heat to which a splash of oil has been added. Do not overcook – just seal until the lamb has a light brown colour all over.

Then, place the lamb in a deep roasting tray, adding half of the lamb stock and making sure it covers the meat. Slow roast the lamb, braising at 150°c (fan) for 3-4 hours until tender.

With around ninety minutes to go, caramelise the onions in a non-stick frying pan, adding some of the lamb stock until brown before reducing until you have a nice glaze.

Peeling and slicing the potatoes to the width of a 50p piece, line a deep baking tray with a layer of them. Add the onion mix as a middle layer, and then cover with the remaining potatoes. Cover with lamb stock (making sure to keep a little for the end), and brush with the melted butter, adding a little more rosemary over the top and bake at 160°c (fan) for an hour.

With half an hour to go before the lamb is cooked, chop the leeks into small rings, adding them and the carrots to the roasting tray. Separately, bake the smoked bacon until crispy.

When the lamb is cooked, remove to rest. Strain the remaining stock into the roasting pan with a sieve. Use the sieve to strain any fat from the top and reduce the stock to make the sauce.

To serve

Serve on the plate with the lamb as the centre-piece with the leeks and carrots piled around it, sauce poured over it and garnished with bacon. Delicious!

Everyone's favourite
DISH!

With a long, illustrious history, an enviable reputation for quality, variety and service, as well as a clear vision for the future, Barkworths Seafood offers the customer a killer triple whammy...

Now Shropshire's largest independent fishmongers, Barkworths has been a trading name in the county and in Shrewsbury for nearly a century. It's a business that stretches back to the time when the company owned and ran its own trawlers to make sure that the very best of the catch found its way to Barkworths name. When it was bought by current owner and director Ian Cornall in 1996 Barkworths faced pressure from the rise of supermarkets and convenience shopping, like many other traditional food outlets at this time. But by focusing on their strengths of quality, variety, and outstanding customer service, and developing new areas of the business under Ian's guidance the last two decades have seen Barkworths go from strength to strength.

The most noticeable of these is the superb Saint Pierre Seafood Bar. Situated directly opposite the main shop in Shrewsbury's famed Market Hall and named after the French term for the John Dory fish, Saint Pierre began as a sideline selling Champagne, oysters, and crab sandwiches on a stall. It has grown to become one of the market's must-stop venues; a vibrant, fresh foodie hotspot, it uses fish fresh from the counter to create an ever-changing range of delicious seafood, salads and soups – all made from scratch in the shop's kitchen.

Of course, for those who want to do their own cooking, Barkworths shop continues to provide the very best quality fresh fish and seafood to both wholesale and retail customers. If you've ever wondered where some of the best chefs around Shropshire source their seafood, well, Barkworths is the answer. The shop supplies some of the restaurants and eateries featured in this very book, such as The Peach Tree and The Haughmond.

The success of the business with daily customers, professionals, and visitors to the restaurant alike is down to an ethos that combines quality and sustainability. Barkworths loves to source fresh fish, and much of what passes over the counter comes directly from small supplies, family-run companies and day-boats.

'Sustainability is a modern buzzword,' explains Ian. 'But the reality is that if everyone bought their fish in its prime seasonal form from a good fishmonger who in turn buys direct from small owner day boats not only do you get the tastiest fish, but there would be plenty more of them in the sea.'

From Cornish oysters and fresh-gathered mussels to seasonal stand-outs like plaice, stone-bass, skate, and black bream Barkworths focus is on plenty of varieties of tasty fish caught predominantly off Britain's coasts. The result is simply the best and widest quality of choice for customers, all delivered with a smile!

SEA FOOD BAR

Barkworths

Barkworths

This dish lends itself to any fish that can be pan-fried or cooked on a griddle. Our favourites are sea bass or sea bream – which are readily available nowadays. The result is a simple, yet tasty dish that makes a perfect lunchtime meal, especially if served with some garlic and rosemary ciabatta and a glass of Sauvignon blanc.

Preparation time: 10 minutes | Cooking time: 8-10 minutes | Serves 2

Ingredients

2 fillets of sea bream or sea bass (approximately 140-180g in weight, scaled and pin-boned)

4 Scottish scallops, roe on

6 raw tiger prawns, peeled

12 cherry tomatoes

1 medium green pepper, chopped

1 medium yellow pepper, chopped

1 lemon

Rosemary, 1 bunch

Flat-leaf parsley, 1 bunch

Fresh thyme, 1 bunch

Olive oil

For the dressing:

Garlic rapeseed oil

White wine vinegar

Maldon sea salt, to taste

Black pepper, to taste

To serve:

Rosemary ciabatta (optional)

Garlic and rosemary potatoes (optional)

Method

To prepare

Begin by chopping the peppers into 2-inch long strips and place into a sauté pan along with the tomatoes. Drizzle in olive oil and season with salt and black pepper. Strip the thyme leaves and toss them in.

Then, pat dry the fish fillets and scallops. This will help them attain their crispness when cooked. Season with salt, pepper and a little rosemary. To make the dressing, mix one part white wine vinegar to three parts garlic rapeseed oil, seasoning with a little salt and pepper.

To cook

Heat a flat griddle or frying pan and pour on some olive oil. Lay the fish fillets skin side down alongside the scallops on a medium high heat. Heat until the skin crisps and the scallops caramelize. Don't be tempted to move them around, but do gently lift to check that this has happened.

At the same time, heat the tomatoes and peppers in the sauté pan. As they come up to heat, throw in the raw prawns and toss the pan or stir for a couple of minutes. Pop the lid on the pan and turn the heat down before allowing to cook through. Then, turn the fish and the scallops and allow to cook for a further 3-4 minutes.

To serve

Tip the tomatoes, peppers and prawns from the sauté pan straight into a large pasta bowl. Then, place the fish fillet on top, skin side up with the scallops surrounding. Drizzle with the dressing, adding the flat leaf parsley, and serve with a lemon wedge and rosemary ciabatta and/or garlic and rosemary roast potatoes.

Go on a
BEAR HUNT!

A warm and welcoming country inn in Shropshire's stunning countryside,
The Bear at Hodnet celebrates good food, good drink and good hospitality...

They say that you can't choose your family, only your friends. Luckily, The Bear at Hodnet has managed to combine both into a must-visit country inn. You see, between landlords Greg and Pia, Thierry, Chris and Sharon, and Jack and Betsy (the dogs) there's something of a well-travelled League of Nations feel to the team. But they've all gelled together into a close-knit family that has made The Bear a wonderfully warm and welcoming experience whether you're just dropping in for a pint, staying for food, or staying over for an evening or two.

The Bear manages the difficult knack of being the sort of place that we all like to visit but rarely seem to find nowadays. The half-timbered building in picturesque Hodnet is surrounded by sumptuous Shropshire countryside and its own gardens – perfect for lazy summer afternoons. Its exposed beams, cosy interior decor, open fires, real ale and good food are the sort of elements that have ticked boxes for guests, visitors and travellers for centuries now. For real ale lovers, the selection is fantastic, featuring a variety of hand-pulled cask ales and guest beers. For oenophiles, the wine list is carefully balanced to complement both the menus and the needs of those who simply would like a glass of wine.

Led by chef Thierry Deliege, the kitchen sits classic pub fare against inventive flavour combinations, offering all that's best and good about modern British cooking. Shropshire is the land of the locally-sourced, and The Bear at Hodnet is no exception. It draws together the best produce available from local suppliers and combines it with a homemade ethos. There are no ready meals here, or microwaves going 'ping!' to indicate that your meal is ready. It's all made onsite, from scratch. Of course, an inn isn't really an inn until it serves a Sunday roast and The Bear's is something special: hearty, full of flavour; perfect whether you need ballast for that long Sunday afternoon walk or whether you did your miles in the morning.

Originally a sixteenth-century coaching inn and located on an old trade route from Shrewsbury to Market Drayton, The Bear has been synonymous with hospitality and accommodation for centuries and it doesn't disappoint in the modern era. There are seven bedrooms, including triple, double and twin and single rooms for overnight breaks. But with lots to do and see nearby, there are plenty of reasons to visit and extend your stay. Oh, and did we mention that the original bear pit is still visible, or that the inn is reputed to be inhabited by eight ghosts...?!

The Bear at Hodnet
SALMON AND COD FISHCAKE WITH SWEDISH BEETROOT SALAD

This simple, easy recipe is a favourite of ours here at The Bear at Hodnet,
combining our European culinary influences and a fresh, mixed garden salad
and tartar sauce to remind us that spring has arrived.

Preparation time: 10 minutes | Cooking time: 10 minutes | Serves 6

Ingredients

For the fish cakes:

500g red potato, skins on

125g salmon

125g cod

25g chives, chopped

25g dill, chopped

100ml dry white wine

Sea salt and cracked black pepper for seasoning

For the beetroot salad:

3 medium-sized cooked beetroot, diced

4½ tbsp mayonnaise

4 ½ tbsp crème fraîche

Sea salt and cracked black pepper, to taste

Method

To make the fish cakes

Placing the potato in a half-full pan of water, raise to the boil and cook until almost soft before removing and allowing to cool. At the same time, poach the fish by covering it in water and simmering over a medium heat for around 10 minutes, or until the fish flakes easily when prodded with a fork. When done, remove from the liquid with a slotted spatula and put to one side, Then shredding the potato into a bowl with the large-holed side of a grater, mix in the flaked fish and fresh herbs until evenly blended, adding sea salt and black pepper to taste. Then, shape into evenly-sized cakes.

To make the beetroot salad

Dice the beetroot into 5mm squares (approx) before combining with the crème fraîche and mayonnaise in a suitable mixing bowl, seasoning well to taste.

Serve with your favourite leaves, and a glass of chilled white wine.

Dream DAYS

The Boathouse, Shrewsbury, takes the perfect waterside location and a perfect approach to hospitality to deliver what might be the perfect riverside venue...

The idea of messing about in boats is ingrained into the British psyche; conjuring as it does images of lazy summer days, cool water, good company and good food. Built around much the same elements, The Boathouse offers a fine alternative to getting your hands on the tiller. That it enjoys a reputation as one of Shrewsbury's best-loved historic pubs is no doubt in part down to its stunning location. Nestled on the banks of the river Severn, it offers breathtaking views of the river and Quarry Park. These can be enjoyed from the waterside terrace and beer garden. Sun-drenched and vibrant in summer, it's a great place to sit and watch the boats and ducks go by while you relax with a drink from the well-stocked bar. Changing with the seasons the Boathouse also offers an antidote to grey winter days or January blues, however, with its cosy interior, merrily burning log fire and oak-beamed interiors.

The menu reflects the very best of pub food. Hearty grills, roasts, and warming desserts might well be the order of the day in winter, headed by chef Lee Maddox the menu takes advantage of Shropshire's fantastic local produce to offer something for everyone all-year round. The Shropshire gold battered haddock fillet is always a popular choice, as are the in-house made burgers and charcoal-cooked steaks. But with beautifully-judged and made-to-order starters, light bites, and sandwiches too alongside a deli board there's enough to service and satisfy any appetite from those calling in with friends to make a night of it, or those dropping in for a whistle-stop break for a snack.

For those looking for something extra-special to mark a celebratory event or landmark occasion, the Boathouse has the Boatshed, a private room. Offering a buffet menu that can be tweaked to suit any event, it stands on the banks of the river and is large enough to hold 30-35 people, making it ideal for birthday parties, christening celebrations or simply just family and friends get-together's.

As you would expect from a place overseen by Jim Littler, the Boathouse brings all of these elements together with friendly, welcoming staff – meaning that there's never been a better time to go for a wander by the river and then check in to watch the world go by...

The Boathouse

The Boathouse
PAN-ROASTED SEA BASS FILLET WITH WARM SALAD OF RED ONION, PLUM TOMATO AND GREEN BEANS

This quick and easy-to-make main course offers the healthiest of healthy eating choices, but is packed with the perfect flavours and textures for summer dining.

Preparation time: 5 minutes | Cooking time: 10 minutes | Serves 4

Ingredients

4 sea bass fillets, skin on

300g extra-fine green beans, topped and tailed

Olive oil, a dash

4 tomatoes, halved

2 red onions, peeled and sliced #

1tbsp demerara sugar

2 cloves garlic, grated

150ml balsamic vinegar

Salt and pepper

Method

Bringing a large pan of salted water to the boil, add the green beans and cook for 2 minutes before removing and plunging into ice-cold water to cool. Then drain and dry on kitchen paper. Scaling, scoring and pin-boning (your fishmonger can do this if you ask) season the sea bass with salt and pepper before rubbing all over with olive oil. Then, place the fillets into a cold, non-stick frying pan before raising this to a medium high heat and covering with a scrunched sheet of wet greaseproof paper. Cook for around 5 minutes. While this is cooking, in another non-stick frying pan add a dash of olive oil and add the halved tomatoes flat side down. Add the demerara sugar and raise to a medium heat, cooking for 3-4 minutes until the tomatoes begin to caramelize. As they cook, add in the grated garlic and balsamic vinegar, reducing until they're sticky. Then, add in the green beans and red onion and heat for a further minute until they're warmed through before seasoning with salt and pepper.

To serve

Place the warm salad into a bowl with the sea bass on top serve immediately.

The Boathouse
GIN-CURED SALMON WITH CELERIAC REMOULADE AND HOMEMADE BLINIS

This classy and sophisticated fish dish packs a flavoursome punch for entertaining and special occasions.

Preparation time: 24 hours | Cooking time: 20-30 minutes | Serves 4

Ingredients

For the gin-cured salmon:

4 oranges, zested

6 lemons, zested

220g dill

320g caster sugar

620g Maldon sea salt

45g juniper berries, crushed

80g black peppercorns, cracked

1 side of salmon, scaled and pin-boned (you can ask your fishmonger to do this)

280ml gin

For the celeriac remoulade:

1 celeriac, peeled and trimmed

25g capers

40g gherkins, finely diced

20g wholegrain mustard

1tsp chopped chives

50g crème fraîche

120g mayonnaise

Salt and pepper, to taste

For the blinis:

14g yeast

350g plain flour

286ml lukewarm milk

2 eggs, separated into yolks and whites

Salt, one pinch

145ml tepid milk

Method

To make the salmon

The salmon needs to be started at least 24 hours before serving, but will keep in the fridge for a week if necessary. Mix the orange and lemon zest, and then add the dill, sugar, salt, crushed juniper berries and cracked black peppercorns before mixing together. Lay a doubled sheet of cling film onto the work bench and spread ⅓ of the salt mix over it so it's the size of the salmon. Laying the salmon skin-side down, cover it with the rest of the salt mix before drizzling the gin evenly over it and then wrapping it up in the cling film. Lay the parcel in a tray and then cover with another tray, placing a weight on top before putting it in the fridge for 24 hours.

To serve

Three hours before you're ready to serve, begin the blinis. In a bowl, make a thin paste out of the yeast, 225g of the flour, and the lukewarm milk. Leave this paste to ferment for 2 hours in a warm place. Then, add the remaining flour, the egg yolks, the pinch of salt and the tepid milk before mixing thoroughly together. Whisk the egg whites until they are in soft peaks and then fold these into the mixture. Leave to ferment for a further 30 minutes.

While this is fermenting, prepare the celeriac. Cut it into wedges before grating over the large holes of a grater into a bowl. Add the capers, whole-grain mustard, chopped chives, crème fraîche and mayonnaise, mix together and add salt and pepper to taste.

Removing the salmon from the fridge, gently wash and brush off the salt mix before patting dry with a clean cloth. Placing on a serving plate or platter, slice thinly, starting at an angle from the tail.

Returning to the blini mixture, heat a non-stick pan over a medium heat. Once it is hot, spoon small amounts of batter into the pan and fry until golden brown, removing as necessary and continuing until all of the mixture has been cooked.

Placing these on a plate, simply serve all three together, allowing guests to add salmon and celeriac remoulade to their fresh blinis according to taste.

Entente CORDIALE

Amid the rolling green fields of Whittern Farm grows a succulent secret...

The blackcurrant harvest on Jo Hilditch's farm is a significant annual event, linking together the four generations of the family who have worked it's land. For the last 140 years the farm's luscious blackcurrants have been harvested every summer. Blackcurrants may well be food and drink's best kept secret. Some of the harvest goes to major brands like Ribena; some to a juicing company; and some for quick freezing. But a significant proportion goes into making Whittern Farm's award-winning White Heron British Cassis. A sumptuous blackcurrant liqueur, it is made by fermenting juice pressed from the freshly picked blackcurrants with Champagne yeast before fortifying the result with vodka and adding a dash of sugar. The result is a rich, intense fruity drink that has become a firm favourite with many of the contributors to this book, such as Apley Farm Shop, Maynard's Farm, and the Riverside Inn at Aymestrey. With a sweet foretaste and sharp lingering kick, British Cassis is a perfect aperitif, adding zest when twisted into summer fizz and bringing decadent luxury to cocktails over long summer nights. Here are a few ways you can use it to pep up your drinks this summer and beyond.

British Royale

To make a variation on the classic Kir Royale, pop a trio of washed blackcurrants in a chilled Champagne flute, add a generous jiggersworth of British Cassis and then top up with Champagne or prosecco for a perfect summer fizz.

The British Bramble

For those looking to pep up the venerable G and T, decant 50ml of your favourite gin along with 25ml of British Cassis and 15ml of lime juice into a cocktail shaker. Add some ice and shake before pouring into a glass of crushed ice, adding a sprig of blackcurrants or a wedge of lime for a lingering finish.

A Country Tale

Finally, take a long glass, frosted for decadence, add a generous dash of British Cassis and ice cubes and top up with cider or perry to make the perfect drink for long summer days.

Café AleOli
SOPRESA ALEOLI

Owner and chef Frances O'Shea brings the authentic taste and vibe of Spain to her stall in Shrewsbury's popular market hall; and serves up a fast, tasty tapas dish that's easy to make but delicious to taste!

"Having lived in Spain for over a decade and fallen in love with its food culture, celebrating both when I moved to Shrewsbury and opened AleOli in 2014 seemed natural. The name combines those of my two children, Alejandro and Olivia, while reflecting Iberian roots. Alioli is, after all, the region's garlic mayonnaise. AleOli serves breakfast and lunch as well as coffee and cake, and offers a place to drop in to brush up on your Spanish! The tapas menu is also a great way to introduce different foods to children as it's based around sharing dishes.

At AleOli we maintain our high quality and authenticity by locally sourcing our produce, mainly from within the market, while the Spanish produce is supplied direct from a specialist supplier who I've known for years!"

Preparation time: 15 minutes | Cooking time: 8 minutes | Serves 4

Ingredients

4 closed cup mushrooms

1 small red onion

1 red pepper

2 chorizo sausages (cooking version) (omit for a vegetarian version of this dish)

4 eggs

8 tbsp olive oil

Salt and pepper to taste

Tomato frito (these are available from AleOli or a Spanish food shop or supplier)

Manchego or cheddar cheese, grated, to taste

Fresh or dried oregano, to taste

4 x tapas dishes (approx 15cm)

Method

Preheat the oven to 190°c before dicing the onion, chorizo, pepper, and mushrooms. Mix together in a bowl ensuring that they are evenly blended and put to one side. Add 1 tablespoon of oil to each tapas dish before cracking 1 egg into each tapas dish. Once this is done, add 2 tablespoons of tomato frito to each dish and then add equal quantities of the onion, chorizo, pepper, and mushroom mixture to each dish. Season well with salt and pepper before grating over as much cheese as you like. Finally, take a pinch of oregano and sprinkle over each dish according to your preferred taste. Check that the oven is up to temperature and place the tapas dishes in the oven for 10 minutes (approx). While this is cooking, toast some fresh artisanal bread. Drizzle the bread with oil or serve plain, according to taste, and then serve immediately when the 10 minutes is up! Simple, and delicious!

Café AleOli

A place in THE COUNTRY

The Castle Hotel is another jewel in Shropshire's enviable crown of fine places in which to stay and dine...

The fact that Shropshire is well-studded with hotels and holiday lets is a testament to the enduring beauty of its countryside and the fantastic range of attractions to suit all tastes and inclinations that the county provides. Dating back to the eighteenth-century, the four gold star AA-graded Castle Hotel is one of its best, however.

Surrounded by panoramic views and set in a charming and quiet edge-of-town square, with the warm and welcoming feel of a traditional coaching inn the Castle Hotel boasts one of the finest hotel gardens in Shropshire; twelve en-suite bedrooms; a choice of three bars; and an oak-panelled restaurant for guests and visitors. The hotel itself specialises in two and three-night leisure breaks – and with good reason. Situated in Bishop's Castle, an unspoilt market town handily close to Shrewsbury and Ludlow, visitors are surrounded on all sides by the South Shropshire hills – a designated Area of Outstanding Natural Beauty that offers some of the best walking routes in the country. Better yet for those who like to share their rambles with friends of the four-legged variety, the castle prides itself on its pet-friendly policy: dogs don't just stay free of charge; they're positively encouraged and welcomed.

The Castle specialises in the sort of food that's becoming a bit of a rarity nowadays: good, modern pub food cooked onsite that's as hearty as it is healthy and flavoursome as it is fresh. But this is simplicity with style – after all, Michelin-starred restaurants in nearby Ludlow and Shrewsbury once outnumbered their counterparts in London. The Castle uses many of the same local suppliers as their starred peers, taking advantage of the fact that Shropshire produces some of the finest provender in the country to put what's local, seasonal, and best in front of customers in a relaxed, convivial ambience. It's a successful approach too, if the customer testimonials are anything to go by.

The bars take a similar approach, hosting guest ales and beers from two of Shropshire's most-renowned breweries: the Six Bells and the Three Tuns (which holds the distinction of being the oldest licensed brewery in the country no less!). For the ale-inclined, brewery tours can also be booked for the full Bishop's Castle experience. For visitors and guests alike, there are cosy spots to relax in after long winter walks and refreshing terraces extending out into the magical gardens for those lazy summer afternoons. All in all, this is one in which you certainly wouldn't mind raising the drawbridge and barricading yourself in for a while...

Castle Hotel

Castle Hotel

HERB & GARLIC CRUSTED RUMP OF WELSH LAMB, MINTED PEA VELOUTÉ & HONEY ROASTED ROOT VEGETABLES

Blending the best traditional ingredients, this succulent dish offers a tasty and highly classy alternative to the standard Sunday roast, or a sophisticated evening meal.

Preparation time: 20 minutes | Cooking time: 30 minutes | Serves 4

Ingredients

1kg lamb rump

For the herb crust:

Mixed herbs, to taste (but rosemary would definitely be recommended)

3-day old bread, 3 slices

3 cloves garlic

Salt, one pinch

Cracked black pepper, one pinch

100g butter, melted

For the minted pea velouté:

2 onions

250g peas, frozen

25g butter, salted

1 tbsp mint sauce, (homemade if possible)

200ml vegetable stock

100ml double cream

Salt and pepper, to taste

For the honey-roasted vegetables:

1 small swede, diced

500g carrots, sliced into batons

500g parsnips, sliced into batons

50g honey

Cooking oil, for roasting

Salt and pepper, to taste

Method

Blend the ingredients for the herb crust in a food processor until they become a fine mix. Brushing the skin side of the lamb with melted butter, dip the lamb into the crumb mix until the skin is covered in the herb crust.

Taking the ingredients for the honey-roasted vegetables, peel and dice the swede before slicing the carrots and parsnips into batons. Place the carrots and swede in a pan before covering in cold water, adding seasoning, and then bring to the boil. Once the pan is boiling add the parsnips and boil for a further five minutes before draining. Place the oil into a roasting tin, add the boiled vegetables, season with salt and pepper, and cover with the honey. Place this to one side.

Preheat the oven to 180˚c, place the crumb dipped lamb on a roasting tray and place in the oven for approximately 30 minutes, allowing it to cook until medium rare.

After fifteen minutes, place the honey-roasted vegetables into the oven with the lamb. These will take approximately 15 to 20 minutes to roast.

Taking the ingredients for the velouté, dice the onions and fry them in the butter until they have softened. Remove into a saucepan and add the peas, mint sauce, vegetable stock, and cream before cooking for a further ten minutes. Then, using a food processor, blitz this mixture until it is smooth. Season with salt and pepper to taste.

Removing the lamb from the oven, allow it to rest for five minutes while the honey-roast vegetables finish. Then, slicing the lamb into 4/5 pieces, drop a spoonful of pea velouté on to the plate and drag across to the other side. Place the lamb on top, and the roasted vegetables around it. Garnish with fresh rosemary and serve immediately.

Castle Hotel
CHOCOLATE & ORANGE BROWNIE
TRAY BAKE & FLOWER POTS

This easy to prepare brownie recipe not only makes superb brownies, but offers a series of variations and additions with which to spice them up into a rich and luxurious dessert.

Preparation time: 30 minutes | Cooking time: 25 minutes | Serves 12

Ingredients

For the tray bake:

375g soft unsalted butter

375g orange chocolate

6 large eggs

1 tbsp vanilla extract

500g caster sugar

225g plain flour

1 tsp salt

For the brownie flower pots:

150g butter or margarine

150g caster sugar

100g self-raising flour

50g cocoa powder

3 medium eggs

200g dark chocolate

125g Chocolate & Orange Brownie (from tray bake) per Brownie Orange

200g white chocolate

Orange food colouring

Skewers

Method

For the tray bake

Preheat the oven to 180°c, melt the butter and chocolate together in a large heavy-based pan. When the chocolate and butter have melted, remove from the heat. While this is cooling, beat the eggs and sugar together with the vanilla extract in the mixer or by hand until smoothly blended together. Then, measure out your flour into a separate bowl, add the salt and set aside.

Once your chocolate mixture has cooled, pour it into the beaten eggs, sugar and vanilla extract mix. Beat this until smooth, sift in the flour, and beat until combined.

Scrape out into a suitable tin and bake for about 25 minutes. The top should have a dry, pale crust while the middle should be nice and gooey. This will make you a basic (but an absolutely fantastic) tray bake Chocolate & Orange brownie, but the following can also be made to complement them.

For the brownie flower pots

To make the soil

Preheat the oven to 180°c, cream the butter and sugar together in a bowl. Sift in the flour and cocoa, add the eggs and mix until completely combined. Placing this into a cake tin, cook for 20 minutes until a skewer comes out clear. Then, set the sponge aside until it is completely cool before crumbling to a soil-like consistency.

To make the chocolate flowerpots

Place the dark chocolate into a heatproof bowl and carefully melt over a pan of simmering water. Take a mini-silicon flower mould and paint the melted chocolate inside the mould with a pastry brush. Then place it into the fridge to set for 30 minutes before carefully peeling off the mould once set. With a pastry brush, dust the outside of the pot with a little cocoa to give the pot a natural look.

To make the icing and brownie oranges:

Blitz 125g of brownie in a food processor until it becomes crumb, then mould into a ball shape, wrap it in cling film and place it into the fridge for 5 minutes. Meanwhile, place the white chocolate into a heatproof bowl and melt over a pan of simmering water. Once melted, add the food colouring until you get the colour you're looking for. Place a skewer into a piece of brownie, dip it into the melted chocolate mix and then stand it upright and place it in the fridge to set.

To serve

Fill the flower pot with chocolate soil and then gently lay the pot on to its side to allow some grains to spill out. Sprinkle dried mixed petals over the soil. Garnish with a mint leaf and clove to give an orange effect.

On the cutting EDGE

Introducing the mysteries and wonders of Oriental steel to amateurs and professionals alike, the Chef's Locker also offers a treasure trove of must-have kit for the kitchen.

Most of us reach into the cutlery drawer or towards the knife block without ever really thinking about it. If we were being honest even the proficient and regular cooks among us might struggle to remember the last time we sharpened and maintained our kitchen knives the way we're supposed to. A quick swipe on the steel before carving, perhaps, but rarely more. The Chef's Locker, which specialises in exquisitely functional high-end Japanese steel, recognizes what every chef worth their salt knows intimately: the knife you choose isn't just the most essential tool in the kitchen. It's an extension of your personality.

Owner Ed had his own road to Damascus steel experience in Barcelona. A working chef for over ten years, he picked up a Japanese-made knife there and never looked back. "Among some of the older generation German knives might still be a first choice," he explains. "But most people who start using Japanese knives never go back. They're something special. I'd say eighty percent of our customers are working chefs. But the twenty percent of those who don't work directly with food is growing – people recognize that they really are something special."

They certainly are. The aesthetic beauty of the hardware that's on offer at the Chef's Locker is something to behold. The patterning on the 'Sakai' Hammered VG10 Damascus Gyuto, created by the core of the knife being 'wrapped' in softer alloys is simply stunning. The forging process, undertaken by highly-skilled craftsmen, involves repeatedly layering and folding the metal, resulting in a blade that holds a seriously sharp edge and keeps it that way for longer. VG10, Shirogami (white carbon steel) and Aogami Super Blue Steel variants are all available across a range of styles. Don't be fooled that these are simply things of beauty. These are tools, designed and engineered to be used. They'll take everything you can throw at them in the kitchen and more.

With chefs moving evermore out of the kitchen in terms of their profile and lifestyle, the equipment that all cooks use reflects something of themselves and their interests. Ed's collection of knives are complemented by a purpose-designed range of knife rolls. Hand-crafted in soft touch leather made from high-grade cow hide and brass fastenings with custom bespoke options available by order these are tools for those who want to make a statement in the kitchen. The range is rounded out by custom-designed racks, with blocks and boards in development. The knives may be at the sharp end, but as a one-stop shop for chefs and cooks alike, the Locker is a good place to rummage!

Their customers include James Close at the 2 Michelin star Raby Hunt, Dinner by Heston at the Mandarin Knightsbridge, Master Chef Winner Gary Maclean and Chris Burt of Momo-No-Ki Ramen.

Chris Burt
CHILLI AND MISO BUTTERED ROASTED DUCK NOODLE SOUP

Shropshire chef Chris Burt puts a modern twist on an oriental classic for those who really fancy a quick take on how to go Japanese.

Preparation time: 10 minutes | Cooking time: 10 minutes | Serves 1

Ingredients

200g roast duck (leftovers are ideal for this)

1 duck egg, free-range if possible

100g soba noodles

1 slice naruto fishcake

2g toasted black sesame

2g shaved katsuobushi

Wild garlic leaves, a bunch (I locally forage these, add quantities to suit personal taste)

½ pint pickled onion juice

Dashi stock, 1 packet

50ml soy sauce

15g shiro (white) miso

15g butter

30g crispy chilli

Method

For the duck

Preheat the oven to 180°c/190°c fan.

When rustling this dish up for myself, I tend to use duck that I've already pre-roasted for other dishes. After all, waste not, want not... Mix the miso, crispy chilli, a dash of soy and the butter together until evenly blended. Rub the mixture evenly on the duck before re-roasting for around ten minutes.

For the dashi

A purist might suggest making the dashi from scratch, but that would introduce the element of hard labour to what is supposed to be an otherwise quick and easy dish! So, pop the kettle on to boil. Once it's boiled and then cooled for three minutes, crack open your dashi powder sachet, and mix up as directed on the packet.

Then add the pickled onion juice, stirring in, before putting it to one side. Keep it hot, though!

For the egg

If I'm working in a professional kitchen when making this, I tend to simply set the Sous-vide to 62°c and add the egg. Job done. However, if you don't have that option, and many of you won't, the best way to approach this is to think boiled egg. Be careful not to overcook it. It needs to be runny...

For the noodles

Filling a pan three-quarter full with water, bring it to a rolling boil before blanching your noodles for 3 minutes. Drain the noodles, and then refresh in cool water before draining again.

To assemble

Add the noodles to the bottom of a favourite bowl. Drop in the dashi. Add the roast duck. Add however much wild garlic you want. Peel the egg and drop it in. Add the toasted sesame. Sprinkle katsuobushi over the whole ensemble, add a slice of naruto fishcake – and enjoy!

Room at
THE INN

Once a traditional country inn, now an award-winning restaurant with rooms,
The Coach House, Norbury, is a place with history, heritage and heart.

Since purchasing The Coach House, Norbury a little over 3 years ago, owners Sean and Lexi Morris have dedicated themselves to creating exactly the kind of place they would like to stay in themselves. An inn has stood on this site since the eighteenth-century, so what they bought was a building with history and character. They've added a friendly welcoming style and laid-back yet attentive service, gorgeously comfortable rooms with luxurious bedding and truly outstanding food complemented by an exciting drinks list. Nestled amid the South Shropshire hills, an Area of Outstanding Natural Beauty whose breathtaking landscapes have inspired poets and artists for generations, it all combines to make The Coach House a venue to visit.

Perfectly situated for walkers and cyclists in the Upper Onny Valley between the towering Stiperstones Ridge and the heathlands of the Long Mynd, the market towns of Ludlow and Shrewsbury are close by too. With several National Trust properties only a short drive away too there is plenty for guests to see and do during their stay.

Open in the evening, the restaurant is overseen by Shropshire born-and-bred chef Harry Bullock. With stints at La Becasse, Fishmore Hall, The Pound at Leebotwood and Le Manoir quat' Saisions under his belt Harry is more than qualified to deliver an exciting and modern seasonal menu. Working closely with the region's best artisan producers the menu changes monthly, and is supplemented by a series of tasting menus throughout the year. Wednesday nights offer a more casual laid-back approach with great value pub food in a wonderfully welcoming atmosphere.

The Coach House, Norbury prides itself on its friendly personal service. Whether visiting with friends or family, or simply passing by, it's the sort of place where you can pull up a chair at one of the wood burning stoves to relax with a drink – whether that means sampling a wine from a carefully selected wine list or one of the locally-made artisanal beers on tap. Having recently scooped an award for the best dog friendly B&B in the country, dogs are more than welcome in both the bar areas and 3 of the 7 letting rooms. As holders of a Visit England Breakfast award for 3 successive years, guests awake after a peaceful night's sleep to a generous breakfast buffet and a locally-sourced cooked breakfast. For those looking for a longer stay there is also a self-catered holiday cottage a few hundred metres away. Cosy and with views out to the Long Mynd, the 2-bedroom Sun Cottage is available to book through The Coach House.

Photo: Sean Morris

Photo: Sean Morris

The Coach House
RHUBARB AND TONKA BEAN PARFAIT

Rhubarb is one of spring's most treasured crops. Grown here at The Coach House, Norbury, we've created a dish that makes it sing!

Preparation time: 6 hours | Cooking time: 1 hour | Serves 4

Ingredients

For the poached rhubarb:

1kg Timperley early rhubarb

1 lemon, unwaxed, zest and juice

100g caster sugar

For the parfait:

75ml double cream

3 egg yolks

75g caster sugar

150g rhubarb purée

1 whole tonka bean

One piping bag

A sugar thermometer

For the macaron:

150g almonds, ground

150g icing sugar

150g caster sugar

120g egg whites (approx. 4 whites)

1 whole tonka bean

A piping bag

For the caramelized and the frozen white chocolate:

200g white chocolate

½ tonka bean

Method

Preheat the oven to 145°c.

For the poached rhubarb

Clean the rhubarb before peeling. Cut the rhubarb into 2cm pieces and place a single layer into a heavy-based pan.

Add the zest and juice of the lemon, the peel, caster sugar and 200ml of water to a pan and bring to a gentle boil. Remove from the heat and strain over the peeled rhubarb. Gently heat this mixture to 60°c and poach for ten minutes until cooked but still firm. Remove from the heat, and reserve half.

To make the parfait

Purée the reserved rhubarb in a food processor. Set aside 150g, and place the rest into a piping bag for plating. Add the double cream to a bowl, whisking to soft peaks. Beat the egg yolks until pale and fluffy. Bring the caster sugar and 35ml of water to the boil on a medium heat. Use a sugar thermometer, heat to 120°c, remove from the heat and gradually whisk in the egg yolks. Continue whisking until cooled and then fold in the semi-whipped cream before adding the remaining purée and a finely-grated whole tonka bean. Ballantine using cling film, and freeze for at least 6 hours.

To make the macaron

Separate 4 eggs. Sift the icing sugar and the ground almonds together and a grated tonka bean. Add half of the egg whites and beat to a thick paste. Leave to rest. Whisk the remaining egg whites in a food mixer on a slow speed. Heat the sugar and 60ml of water and bring to 120°c. Increase the food mixer's speed to create stiff peaks and when the sugar reaches the correct temperature, remove from the heat and whisk in the egg whites, continuing as it cools. Use a spatula to beat ⅓ of the meringue into the almond mixture before folding in the rest. Place into a piping bag, pipe 2cm diameter circles onto a flat sheet of baking parchment, leaving space for spreading. Set aside to dry for 1 hour before placing in the oven for 13-15 minutes. They're cooked when you can lift one cleanly from the parchment without leaving residue. Allow to cool, then place in an airtight container.

For the caramelized white chocolate

Reducing the oven temperature to 120°c add 100g of broken chocolate onto a silicone tray liner and melt in the oven for 25 minutes. At 5 minute intervals, remove and agitate with a palette knife. Once the chocolate is golden, remove, and allow to cool for 3 hours before shredding with a sharp knife and storing in an airtight container.

For the frozen white chocolate

Melt the remaining chocolate over a bain-marie. Once melted, spread thinly over a sheet of baking parchment and grate over a sprinkling of tonka bean. Freeze for at least 2 hours.

To serve

Place some of the caramelized chocolate onto a plate followed by the rhubarb purée. Filling a macaron with some Chantilly cream, stabilize this on the plate with the rhubarb purée. Cut the parfait into 2cm sections and arrange on the plate. Drain the poached rhubarb, and add to the plate. Add the white chocolate shards, and serve!

A place for
ALL SEASONS

In the foodie heaven that is Shrewsbury, four brothers have come together to offer something a little different...

The antics of the likes of Marco Pierre-White and Gordon Ramsay have painted the professional kitchen as a gladiatorial ring in which professional chefs participate in a full-contact blood sport. Now, throw in that the course of family life rarely runs smooth and you might think that four brothers opening their own restaurant might be a recipe for disaster. But Reuben, Adam, Ben, and Josh Crouch have taken their lifelong passions for good food and well-travelled personal histories and stirred it up to create CSons: a fresh, funky addition to Shrewsbury's food scene.

It works so well because as in all recipes it's all about the blend. Reuben has brought a wealth of retail experience including seven years as General Manager at the multi-award winning Ludlow Food Centre to CSons' marketing side. As CSons' front-of-house manager, Adam draws upon his experiences at some of the UK's best-known eateries to make guests feel welcome at any time of the day or night. Josh brings an impressive track record, including five years as Clive Davis's right-hand man at the Michelin-listed Green Café, to his role as head chef. In this he's ably supported by brother Ben, a man

who has been in the trade all of his working life, including a stint as head chef at East London's renowned Pavilion Café alongside Brett Redman.

The food takes advantage of Shropshire's enviable local produce, but while it's globally-inflected, reflecting the travelling the brothers have done, it also refreshingly places a wonderful emphasis on using lesser-known staples to create inspired affordable food. Think slow-cooked brisket rather than flash-grilled fillet. The ethos is simple and unpretentious to showcase the seasonal flavours of the ingredients perfectly.

The exceptional food is matched by the surroundings. Shrewsbury has no shortage of buildings with a history, but back in the sixteenth-century CSons restaurant was the Sun Tavern and the grade-II listed building has retained beautiful Tudor wall panelling, a seventeenth-century staircase, and the ornate period mantel above the fireplace. With its enclosed courtyard garden CSons has been finished with a light, airy feel and its character matches that of the menu and its owners perfectly. In other words, it's a perfect place to visit for breakfast, lunch, or dinner and feel perfectly at home in!

CSons

PURPLE SPROUTING BROCCOLI WITH POLENTA, MUHAMARRA, POACHED EGG AND PARMESAN

Like all the food at CSons this dish is locally sourced but globally inspired. The muhamarra and spiced oil add a fresh twist on a classic Italian dish, and is best made when the broccoli is local and in season!

Preparation time: 20 minutes | Cooking time: 1 hour | Serves 6

Ingredients

For the broccoli:

500g purple sprouting broccoli

3 garlic cloves

Parsley, handful

100g butter

For the Muhamarra:

6 roasted, peeled and deseeded red peppers

100g fresh breadcrumbs

1 tbsp lemon juice

2 tbsp pomegranate molasses

3 tsp ground cumin

2 tbsp dried Aleppo chilli flakes

2 small garlic clove, peeled, crushed

100g walnuts, finely chopped by hand

4 tbsp olive oil, plus extra to finish

For the polenta:

110g polenta

800ml milk

200ml cream

100g grated Parmesan

100g unsalted butter

For the poached eggs:

6 eggs, fresh, free-range

100 ml white wine vinegar

180g shaved Parmesan

To serve:

100 ml olive oil

1 tsp smoked paprika

Method

Start by preparing the broccoli. Fill a pan large enough to fit all of the broccoli into full of water and add a teaspoon of salt. Bring it to the boil, cook the broccoli for 2 minutes before placing in ice-cold water. Once it's cool, set aside.

Then make the muhamarra. Place all the ingredients into a food processor and blend until all the ingredients are combined. Check the consistency. If it seems a little dry, add an extra dash of olive oil. Add seasoning to taste and put to one side.

Turning your attention to the polenta, bring the milk and cream nearly to a boil over a medium heat. Then, slowly whisk in the polenta. Add a little at a time so that it doesn't stick together and then carry on whisking until it thickens to the consistency of double cream. Then lower the heat and cook for around 30-40 minutes until the grainy texture is no longer there. Remember to whisk sporadically so that the polenta doesn't catch.

When the polenta is nearly done, turn your attention to the poached eggs. Bring a large pan of water to the boil and add the vinegar. Take off the heat and then quickly and carefully crack the eggs into the water as close to the waterline as possible. Return the pan to the heat and then poach for three minutes.

Finely chop the garlic and parsley together and set aside. Then, mix the olive oil and smoked paprika together and set aside.

Heat a frying pan, add the 100g of butter and toss the cooked broccoli into the butter, adding in the chopped garlic and parsley.

Then, just before serving the polenta, whisk in the butter and grated Parmesan.

To serve

This is best served in a bowl. Spoon the polenta into the bottom before adding the broccoli and the muhamarra. Finish with the poached egg, adding Parmesan and the paprika oil before serving. Add a nice glass of Shiraz to accompany!

Covering the BASES

The Loopy Shrew, PorterHouse and Darwin's Townhouse offer something for everyone...

Sometimes what you need is hearty, flavoursome food delivered with a smile. You may want to try something à la carte, or maybe paint the town red? Cocktails could be on the menu, perhaps something light, zesty, and fresh to set you up for the evening ahead. Then again, we all occasionally enjoy some time to ourselves, whether that's a relaxed cup of coffee or a longer weekend break to refresh ourselves.

Luckily, locals and visitors to Shrewsbury have their choice covered by The Loopy Shrew, PorterHouse and Darwin's Townhouse. Owned by The DiTella Group, a family business headed by Ann DiTella, Mark Davies and Danielle DiTella. All three venues share the same elegantly-appointed tasteful style and commitment to exceptional food and service, each offering a different experience.

The Loopy Shrew excels as a wine bar serving food, with the option of staying over in charming individual rooms. The breakfast, lunch and evening menus are based around local produce and suppliers, such as Hall, Wenlock Edge Farm, Moyden's Cheese and Swift's Bakery. From hearty staples or light bites to something sumptuous for a special occasion, this is a place that you could easily drop into with friends for a drink or you could host a family celebratory event in, especially with the option for a private dining experience available.

PorterHouse covers the American end of the spectrum, serving food that's packed with flavour: juicy burgers, handmade daily to a secret recipe; succulent chicken wings; and perfect steaks are the order of the day, with everything made on-site daily from the best local produce. With an airy light conservatory, or an intimate cosy restaurant to choose from, and attentive, friendly waiting staff throughout this is the perfect place for those who want to make a night of it – with the option of relaxing into blissful sleep in one of their four boutique rooms.

Finally, Darwin's Townhouse, a late-eighteenth century Grade-II listed Georgian townhouse offers a twenty-bedroom boutique bed and breakfast in the heart of Shrewsbury. Completely refurbished to the highest standards in 2016, Darwin's boasts rooms from beautiful singles to sumptuous suites. This is a place to stretch out and relax in, perhaps with a cup of fresh coffee or tea in one of the snugs or in the private courtyard and secret garden – exclusively kept for guests.

So, whether you're passing through or staying awhile, between The Loopy Shrew, PorterHouse, and Darwin's there's no need to look much further...

The DiTella Group

DARWIN'S
TOWNHOUSE

BOUTIQUE
BED & BREAKFAST

THE LOOPY SHREW

PORTER HOUSE

Darwin's Townhouse

PROPER EGGS BENEDICT

Darwin's Townhouse puts together the best way to serve up this luxurious breakfast staple.

Preparation time: 20 minutes | Cooking time: 15 minutes | Serves 1

Ingredients

1 English breakfast muffin

1 plum tomato

2 slices of roast ham

2 fresh eggs, free-range

Baby watercress

1 tbsp cracked black pepper

For the hollandaise sauce:

4 fresh free-range eggs, separated

1 block of unsalted butter

2 tbsp white wine vinegar

Salt, pinch

Method

To make the hollandaise

Crack and separate the eggs, add the egg yolks and white wine vinegar into a steel mixing bowl and then whisk over a saucepan of simmering water until slightly thickened before removing from the heat. Melt the butter in a separate saucepan, slowly add the egg mixture, whisking constantly to avoid any lumps. If the hollandaise begins to thicken, add a couple of spoonfuls of boiling water to thin it out. Season with salt to taste and remove from the heat.

Toast the breakfast muffin, place on a plate, and add 2 slices of plum tomato and 1 slice of roast ham to each half. In a pan of simmering water, crack both eggs and cook for 2 ½ minutes exactly. Then, take the eggs out with a perforated spoon and place 1 on each half of the muffin. Spoon the hollandaise on top of the eggs before seasoning with cracked black pepper and garnish with baby watercress before serving immediately.

The Loopy Shrew

LOOPY'S FAMOUS SCOTCH EGG

The Loopy Shrew shows you how to make the perfect hangover cure, breakfast, and savoury snack.

Preparation time: 1hr 20 minutes | Cooking time: 15 minutes | Serves 5

Ingredients

For the Scotch egg:

5 free-range eggs

1 tube of sausage meat

1 tsp of grain mustard

1 tsp of English mustard

1 cup of fresh breadcrumbs

½ cup of fresh chopped parsley

For the breadcrumb coating:

3 free-range eggs

1 cup of plain flour

2 cups of dried breadcrumbs

For the garnish:

Loose leaf salad

Local piccalilli

Method

To make the Scotch egg

Gently place the eggs in a pan of boiling water and cook for 5 minutes. Then remove the eggs and run under cold water for 5 minutes. Peel the eggs, discard the shells and put to one side. In a bowl, mix together the sausage meat, English mustard, grain mustard, fresh breadcrumbs and parsley until evenly blended. Then roll this mixture into balls roughly the same size as the eggs before flattening them out. Gently wrap the eggs in the sausage meat and then place in the fridge for 30 minutes. If necessary, use a drop of cold water to help move the meat around the eggs.

To make the breadcrumbs

In 3 separate shallow containers, place 3 whisked eggs, 1 cup of plain flour and the dried breadcrumbs. Taking the Scotch eggs out of the fridge, roll them gently in the flour container. Then dip the Scotch eggs into the egg mix and shake off any excess before rolling them gently in the breadcrumb container and then chill in the fridge for a further 20 minutes.

Preheat the oven to 180˚c degrees and a deep fat fryer to 175˚c degrees. Deep fry the Scotch eggs until golden, and then oven bake them for 6 minutes. Serve with a small salad and piccalilli.

PorterHouse
ULTIMATE PULLED PORK BURGER

PorterHouse adds taste, texture and variation to a much-loved classic in their take on the mighty burger.

Preparation time: 24 hours | Cooking time: 6 hours | Serves 8

Ingredients

For the pulled pork:

2kg pork shoulder

1 litre of ginger beer

1 cup of brown sugar

½ cup of smoked paprika

¼ cup of cumin

¼ cup of ground ginger

½ cup of cajun spice

¼ cup of salt

¼ cup of cracked black pepper

For the burger:

2kg mince beef

2 tbsp of Marmite

2 tbsp of English mustard

1 tbsp of horseradish sauce

For the BBQ sauce:

Braising juice from the pork shoulder

½ litre of tomato ketchup

¼ cup of honey

½ cup of brown sugar

2 tbsp of smoked paprika

Also:

8 rashers of streaky bacon

8 brioche buns

4 tbsp mayonnaise

4 beef tomatoes, chopped

Gem lettuces

Method

To make the pork

Mix together the brown sugar, smoked paprika, cumin, ground ginger, Cajun spice, salt and cracked black pepper to make the BBQ rub for the pork shoulder. Rub this over the pork shoulder and leave it to marinate for 24 hours. After 24 hours, preheat the oven to 150°c degrees. Placing the pork in a deep tray, add the ginger beer before covering it with foil. Place it in the oven and slow cook for 5 hours.

After 5 hours, remove the pork from the oven and then drain the liquid into a large saucepan. Shred down the pork into a separate bowl and put to one side. To the leftover liquid, add the ketchup, brown sugar, honey and paprika, and then simmer over a medium heat for 30 minutes until reduced to a sauce. After 30 minutes add the shredded pork back to the sauce and then stir well.

To make the beef burger

Mix the minced beef, marmite, English mustard and horseradish in a bowl until evenly blended and then divide it into 8 burgers. Cook them and the bacon either in the oven or under the grill (according to taste).

When the burgers are cooked, slice the brioche buns in half and toast them. Add the mayonnaise, shredded gem lettuce, and beef tomato to the buns, and then place the cooked burgers on top before generously adding the pulled pork and a slice of streaky bacon. Serve with coleslaw, crispy fries or salad according to taste.

Magnum OPUS!

Fine dining, fine accommodation, and much, much more makes The Haughmond a must-visit venue...

We all like word of mouth recommendations. After all, if those we know put us in the know, we feel we're in safe hands. But if that is backed up with award-winning critical acclaim, well, it's hard to go wrong. The Haughmond, a modern coaching inn in the picturesque village of Upton Magna, combines a glowing reputation among customers with a slew of awards, including 2 AA rosettes, Hardens, Michelin Food and Good Hotel Guide listings, celebrating the culinary excellence and outstanding accommodation it offers.

The Haughmond specialises in serving the best locally-sourced produce in creative menu combinations and providing great service in a welcoming environment. Those looking for something special will find much to enjoy in the 'Basil's Taster' menu, an exquisite celebration of the best seasonal ingredients Shropshire has to offer. Following the same ethos, the dinner menu takes a creative approach to the classics: a sumptuous wild boar wellington, for example, served with roast pear, chestnuts, mushrooms and a blue cheese bon bon. Even just popping in for lunch or coffee at the Brassiere, however, there are beautifully-judged light and à la carte menus available. The menus regularly change to accommodate the best ingredients at their peak – so repeat visits are very much the order of the day!

For those seeking something a little more intimate, special, or celebratory, Basil's Dining Room provides an exclusive private dining experience for up to twenty people – not only can the menu be designed for the occasion in conjunction with chef Martin, but he will be your dedicated chef for the evening, as will the waiting staff, ready to tend to your every need. With sumptuous accommodation available too, there's no excuse not to relax back into the lap of luxury and make a night of it either...

You can also take the taste of Haughmond home with you; bespoke hampers are available for private and corporate clients alike. Each can be made up to your specifications, and then sent packed with the finest produce Shropshire has to offer direct to your door.

A real jewel in Shropshire's foodie crown, then, the Haughmond is something special indeed...

The Haughmond
BREAST OF PIGEON WITH SCOTCHED QUAIL'S EGG

This recipe can serve as an impressive starter, or when doubled-up with dressed leaves and fresh bread a hearty lunch. Here at The Haughmond we buy locally. Our pigeons come from the local shoot, our quail's eggs from Attingham Park, our black pudding from Whitchurch, parsnips from Bruckshaw's Farm, and our herbs are from our own garden. However, a good game butcher should certainly be able to help you source what's needed...

Preparation time: 15 minutes | Cooking time: 40 minutes | Serves 4

Ingredients

Vegetable or rapeseed cooking oil

2 parsnips

1 shallot

50ml chicken stock

50ml water

200ml double cream

For the black pudding purée:

100g black pudding

50ml port

50ml red wine

2 sprigs thyme

110g butter

For the pistachio crumb:

160g pistachio nuts

2 cloves garlic

1 star anise

30g breadcrumbs

1 sprig of rosemary

For the Scotch eggs:

4 quail's eggs

75g haggis

75g sausage meat

1 nutmeg

3 eggs

1tbsp flour

4 pigeon breasts

Seasoning, coarse sea salt and cracked black pepper to taste

Method

To make the parsnip purée

Heat a splash of oil in a non-stick pan. Peel and dice the shallot and the parsnips and brown off in the hot oil. Add the chicken stock and the water before cooking over a medium heat. When tender, remove from the heat, season well, and blend together to a creamy consistency. Add a little cream if necessary.

To make the black pudding purée

Preheat the oven to 140°c, place the black pudding, thyme, Port and red wine into an oven proof dish. Cover with a lid and place it in the oven for 1 hour. Remove, add 50g of the butter, and then blitz with a blender, adding seasoning to taste.

To make the pistachio crumb

Turn the oven up to 160°c, place pistachios, cloves, star anise and a handful of the breadcrumbs into a blender before blitzing for a few seconds until broken and mixed, but still reasonably rough. Picking the rosemary from the stalk, roughly dice, and add to the mixture. Pour this onto a baking tray and roast for six minutes.

To make the Scotch quail's egg

Bringing a pan of water to the boil. Drop the quail's eggs into the water and cook for 2 minutes. Remove the eggs and place in cold water to stop them cooking further. When cool, peel, and set aside. Mix together the sausage meat, haggis, grated nutmeg, and seasoning. Split the mix into quarters, flatten and then wrap it around the peeled eggs evenly. Breaking the eggs into a bowl, beat with a fork and then coat the sausage and egg in flour, then in egg, and then in a good coating of breadcrumbs. Add oil to a frying pan, deep fry the Scotch eggs for 2 minutes before removing the oil and leaving to rest.

To make the pigeon breast

Put a splash of oil into a non-stick frying pan on a high heat. When the oil starts to smoke, add the pigeon breasts skin side down. Season well. Leave skin side down for 1 minute approximately before adding a knob of butter to brown. Flip the breast over and carry on cooking for approximately forty-five seconds. Remove from the pan and set aside to rest for 2-3 minutes in a warm place.

To serve

Slice the breast in half sideways and place next to the purées. Cut the Scotch egg in half and place alongside the breasts. Sprinkle a good handful of pistachio crumb around half of the dish. Serve and enjoy!

(A Valpolicella Ripasso ideally pairs with this rich starter. An Italian red, it's excellent with most game dishes!)

Living HISTORY

One of Shrewsbury's favourite venues, Henry Tudor House is independent and family run, offering stylish modern hospitality alongside its atmospheric period charm...

If the first bite is with the eye (and all good chefs suggest that it is), then visitors to Henry Tudor House know they're in line for something special. Coming in off the cobbled street outside, the attractive half-timbered venue is one of the oldest in Shrewsbury. This house was already celebrating its half-century when Henry Tudor spent the night there before a victory at the Battle of Bosworth in 1485 saw him crowned King Henry VII on the battlefield. It radiates period charm, but inside contemporary touches blend sympathetically and stunningly with its rich history.

Beautifully lit, with ever-changing colours reflecting off the long zinc bar the venue houses an oak-framed restaurant; a private dining room for those seeking something a little more intimate and exclusive; an elegant conservatory offering a light and airy feel; and finally a vaulted function room that has won numerous awards for its live music and comedy. Henry Tudor House, is the sort of place you can drop into on the spur of the moment or visit as part of a long-planned occasion with family and friends and be guaranteed a memorable experience every time.

They approach flavours in a similar way at Henry Tudor House. Both the Classic and Signature menus on offer are grounded in rich traditions while embracing the new. This means that the kitchen, led by head chef Paul Downes and overseen by exec chef Chris Conde, a Masterchef quarter-finalist, taps into the rich bounty of Shropshire's best local producers, following the flow of the seasons to put what's best at any given moment right in front of you. The hearty and familiar is on offer, but so are the modern touches and flavour combinations that make meals worth lingering over. This is food made by people who love food and like nothing better than serving up something special, with a generous helping of warm and friendly service, topped with fantastic ambience.

The wine follows Henry Tudor House's ethos of matching the right approach with the right moments. As with the decor and the menus, it's about focusing in on the details to serve the bigger picture. This is why when they were looking for the perfect fizz, the powers that be sent someone into France's Epernay region to find a family rather than corporately produced Champagne to make sure it was perfect.

Add in that Henry Tudor House is available for the big moments in life, offering intimacy in the restaurant, sophistication in the private dining room, and the chance to go wild in the bar or the venue's 'Big Room' and it is clear that we're talking about a pretty special place here. After all, it is practically by Royal Appointment...

Henry Tudor House

SPRING LAMB RACK, BROAD BEAN AND MINT HUMMUS WITH FONDANT POTATO AND CHICKEN JUS

Here at Henry Tudor House we're always looking to add a fresh spin on the classics. This lamb recipe is a perfect spring dish as the nights grow longer and the weather grows warmer.

Preparation time: 10 minutes | Cooking time: 70 minutes | Serves 4

Ingredients

For the chicken jus:

1kg chicken wings

2 cloves garlic

1 sprig fresh thyme

500ml water

200ml white wine

For the fondant potato:

4 large baking potatoes

75g butter

200ml vegetable stock

For the lamb:

2 x 4 bone lamb racks

For the hummus:

250g broad beans

¼ fresh mint, bunch (leaves only, stalks discarded)

2 garlic cloves, peeled

½ lemon, juiced

75ml rapeseed oil

Salt, to taste

For the salsa:

Marjoram, 10 leaves

2 plum tomatoes, deseeded and diced

150g garden peas, fresh

Asparagus, 1 bunch, cut into sections

50ml rapeseed oil

Salt, to taste

Method

To make the chicken jus, which will take the longest amount of time, roast off the chicken wings in the oven until browned and then transfer to a pan. Add the other ingredients and cover the bones with water before gently simmering for 1 hour (approx). Then pass the stock through a sieve before reducing to a glossy consistency.

Turning attention to the fondant potato, peel the potatoes and cut into discs using a cookie cutter. Then gently colour both sides in a frying pan before adding butter and stock and cooking at 180°c for 20 minutes.

While these are cooking, season the lamb before placing it into a medium hot pan fat side down and rendering the fat. Then, remove and place in the oven at 160°c for around 10 minutes. A medium-rare consistency is what is being aimed for. Then remove the lamb from the oven and allow it to rest before carving.

Whilst the lamb is resting, put all of the ingredients for the broad bean hummus into a food processor and purée until a smooth consistency has been achieved. Then, turning attention to the salsa, cook the peas and asparagus in boiling salted water for 2 minutes before refreshing in cold water. Add to the rest of the salsa ingredients and gently warm through the salsa before serving.

To serve

Place a generous spoonful of the hummus onto each plate before adding the fondant potato. Lean the carved lamb racks against the potato and spoon over the salsa before finishing with the chicken jus.

In the FAMILY

A multi-award winning, family-run concern, Hundred House is simply a delight...

You can tell when something is made with love. It can be as simple as a cup of tea in the morning made by a loved one, but you just know that there's a unique combination of heart and head behind it. So it is with Shropshire's award-winning Hundred House. This particular labour of love started on a cold February day in 1985. Having pioneered the gastro-pub idea at The Greyhound, Bicester, Henry and Sylvia Philips viewed a property in a sorry state in need of some serious TLC. They took it on, opening the bar first in July 1985, and then the restaurant the same summer. Even then, the continuing renovation of the rooms above meant cleaning the restaurant assiduously every morning to remove the dust from the building works.

But it was worth it, for Hundred House has been firing on all cylinders ever since, fuelled by the passion, heart, and craft of the whole family. David, a pioneering micro-brewer who became the youngest brewer in Britain in 1981, remains responsible for the hotel's impressive beer and wine lists. Stuart is in charge of the kitchen, returning to Hundred House in 1992 after spells at The Chester Grosvenor, Kensington Place and Le Goven, a Michelin-starred Breton seafood restaurant. In fact, so determined to become a chef was Stuart that he cycled from Oxford to Brittany to work in the latter, sleeping in ditches along the way, and carrying

no more than a few francs in his pocket and his knife roll. They turned him down initially, before hiring him when they realised how determined he was. That determination was rewarded by Hundred House's first AA award of 2 rosettes in 1996. Jo, Stuart's wife, has joined the team, working as General Manager. The award-winning gardens were laid out by Sylvia and remain a monument to her passing, reflecting the love and energy she poured into making Hundred House a delightful and beautiful place for its visitors and guests. Indeed, its herbs, vegetable patch and orchard supply the kitchen to make sure the food is as fresh as it can be.

And what food it is Hundred House's dining has held 2 AA rosettes for 20 consecutive years (and won 'Best Restaurant' category in the Shropshire Star three years in a row as well as this year's What's On Awards 'Best Independent Restaurant in Telford') by serving fantastic pub grub and à la carte menus alike that simply make the best of Shropshire's stunning local produce. Changing with the seasons, these menus hit the spot for those dropping in for lunch, those who wish to make an evening of it, and the hundreds of wedding guests who've found Hundred House's seventeenth-century Tithe Barn and warm hospitality the perfect venue for the most important of days.

Hundred House

ROAST LAMB CUTLET, BRAISED BELLY AND KIDNEY CROQUETTE WITH ROAST ONION PURÉE

At Hundred House we use the best of what's fresh and locally-available. This includes our own herb, fruit, and vegetable gardens, as well as the Apley estate's 2-acre Victorian walled-garden, and our fantastic butcher, Keith Alderson's of Bridgnorth. This recipe brings all of those elements together.

Preparation time: 8 hours | Cooking time: 20-30 minutes | Serves 4

Ingredients

For the lamb cutlet:

A cutlet rack of lamb

For the braised belly of lamb:

1 lamb belly

2 cloves garlic, crushed

1 oz fresh breadcrumbs

2 tbsp parsley, chopped

1 lemon, zested and juiced

Rosemary, 1 sprig

Salt and pepper, to taste

White wine and lamb stock (to deglaze)

Capers & sprigs of Tarragon to finish

For the kidney croquette:

3 lamb's kidneys

250g belly pork, minced

2 tsp thyme and seasoning

Flour, a peck

1 egg

Breadcrumbs

For the roast onion purée:

2 onions

1 medium potato, sliced

½ pint milk

Salt and pepper

Method

To make the braised belly of lamb

In a bowl, mix together the garlic, the breadcrumbs, chopped parsley, lemon zest and juice and rosemary. Cut the belly of lamb in half and then rub over the garlic mixture, seasoning well with salt and pepper. Roll into a cylinder approximately 2 inches by 7 inches and tie with butcher's string. Place this into a vacuum pack and seal tightly. Raising a water bath or saucepan of water to 85°c, cook for 8 hours and then let it cool and set before dividing it into 8mm thick slices.

To make the kidney croquette

Dice the lamb's kidneys to 3mm cubes and then season and sauté in very hot oil for 2 minutes before allowing them to cool. Then mix these with the minced belly pork, thyme, and seasoning. Roll into a croquette shape before rolling in the flour, egg and breadcrumbs. Chill in the fridge until required.

To make the roast onion purée

Peeling and quartering 2 onions, char these over a grill before roasting in a hot oven until golden and tender. Meanwhile, slice 1 medium potato and then poach it in ½ pint of milk until tender. Then season and purée together with the onion.

To cook and serve

Preheat the oven to 200°c. Take the cutlet rack of lamb and season well with salt and pepper. Seal the rack in a hot pan before roasting in the oven for 6-8 minutes. The meat should be pink at the end of cooking. Then rest in a warm oven for ten minutes. While this is resting, take a slice of lamb belly and heat under a hot grill. Warm the onion purée and seasonal vegetables, and deep-fry the kidney croquette for several minutes until hot right through. Deglaze the roasting pan from the lamb rack using the lamb stock and the wine, reducing to a light syrup, adding a few capers and the tarragon.

To serve

Place hot garnish around the plate, cut the rack in to two pieces on top of the hot garnish and spoon around the sauce. Add the slice of belly, kidney croquette, purée, and seasonal vegetables as shown in the photograph and serve immediately.

This girl CAN!

From her cookery courses to her spice range, Sabrina Zeif is bringing eclecticism, fun and connection back to the kitchen...

There are many ways to get to Shropshire, but few are as winding as the course that Kitchen Thyme owner and founder Sabrina Zeif plotted. It's taken her from Trinidad to San Francisco via Texas and New Orleans. All the while, the idea of starting her own business nagged away at her.

Enter Shropshire, a life-change, and the chance to start Kitchen Thyme. Sabrina explains, "Because of my Trinidadian background, I see food as the perfect vehicle to bring people together. Trinidad is incredibly culturally diverse, and its cooking is rooted in community, socialising and authentic flavours".

Kitchen Thyme offers the opportunity for Sabrina to share her international experience and her deep understanding of flavours. This comes in the form of bespoke cookery courses and a delicious spice range.

Kitchen Thyme's courses focus on how to blend spices and herbs to invigorate everyday food using locally sourced ingredients. In each instance, clients are taught to cook exquisite, delicious and fresh homemade dishes bursting with unique flavour and authenticity and they can expect to laugh, relax, and enjoy the learning process along the way.

The spice range has been lovingly developed by Sabrina, drawing on influences from around the globe. They include a Cajun Seasoning, Caribbean Herb Rub and Pulled Meat Rub with the aim to make everyday cooking easy and flavourful.

A one woman tour-de-force ably supported by her development chef, Chris Scarratt, Sabrina's approach to cooking reflects her approach to life: both are things to be celebrated and savoured! It's an approach that has served her well and won many plaudits. But this is just the beginning. With appearances on Simply Good Food TV and the chef stage at Car Fest 2017 already booked, the sky would appear to be the limit…

To book a cookery course or buy Kitchen Thyme products visit www.kitchen-thyme.co.uk.

Kitchen Thyme
COUNTRYSIDE CARIBBEAN BBQ

To create the mouth-watering aromas and rich full flavours of the Caribbean right here in Shropshire, and in your home, the secret is in the seasoning, the marinating, and the use of fresh ingredients...

Preparation time: 24 hours | Cooking time: 20-30 minutes | Serves 8 people (or 4 hungry ones)

Ingredients

For the lamb:

2 x 300g boned rack of lamb, separated

2 tsp thyme

1 tsp ground cumin

½ tsp nutmeg

For the chicken:

4 chicken thighs (bone in)

1 tsp coriander, parsley and spring onion, chopped

½ tsp each garlic and ginger, chopped

1 tbsp soy sause

¼ tsp saffron

(or 2tbsp Kitchen Thyme Herb Rub)

For the prawns:

8 tiger prawns, unpeeled

½ tsp paprika and black pepper

1 tbsp coriander, chopped

3 cloves garlic, crushed

2 tbsp soy sauce and olive oil

(or 2 tsp Kitchen Thyme Cajun Seasoning)

For the pork:

1 x 350g pork loin fillet

1 tsp smoked paprika

½ tsp cumin, black pepper and salt

(or 2 tbsp Kitchen Thyme Pulled Meat Rub)

For the BBQ sauce:

125 ml each soy sauce and ketchup

50 ml mustard

1 tsp coriander, parsley and garlic, chopped

1 tbsp brown sugar

1 chilli pepper, chopped (optional)

1 tsp Kitchen Thyme cajun seasoning

Method

Using three wide shallow dishes, prepare the seasoning marinades. For the lamb, blend all of the spices together, cover each lamb cutlet with the mixture and set aside. For the chicken, mix the herbs, ginger, garlic, saffron, and soy sauce together to make a paste. Carefully cover each piece of chicken in the mixture and set aside. For the prawns, combine all the wet and dry seasonings, cover each prawn in the mixture and set aside. For the pork, rub the mixed seasoning into the pork generously and set aside. The longer you let the meat marinate before cooking, the better the flavours. This can be done 1 day in advance if stored in the refrigerator.

As per recipe notes, you can easily swap the marinade ingredients for Kitchen Thyme's ready-made seasonings to make the process quicker and easier.

To make the BBQ sauces

Mix all of the ingredients together in a saucepan and heat on low for 5 minutes. Add 1 tsp Kitchen Thyme Cajun Seasoning for extra flavour. Set aside while you light the BBQ to a high heat.

Cooking the meat

Once the BBQ is hot, turn the temperature to medium. If using coals, wait until the flames have died down. Add the chicken to the grill and baste with some of the BBQ sauce. Cook for 35 minutes or until juices run clear, turning often. Ten minutes before the chicken is cooked, add the lamb and pork to the grill. Cook each fillet for 5 minutes on both sides or until done. Just before serving, add the prawns to the grill for 3 minutes, turning often. Take all the meat off together. If you can't fit them all on at once, you can also cook them separately.

A Family AFFAIR

One of the jewels in Shrewsbury's foodie crowns, La Dolce Vita is pushing the boundaries of what we think of as Italian cuisine...

It's easy to forget that Italian food is the world's favourite. In Britain, Indian cuisine tends to top the lists in surveys alongside national staples like the Full English or the Sunday Roast. But that's because we've come to take Italian food almost for granted – and that's a tribute to the way that it's become part of the everyday language of our lives and an essential part of our food experiences.

Even for someone born into an Italian foodie family, for Gennaro Adaggio, the lightbulb moment didn't happen until he was fifteen. 'I'd always enjoyed good food,' he explains. 'But it wasn't until I set foot in a professional kitchen that things clicked into place. From that moment on, food became a passion.' It was a passion that led him through multiple Michelin-starred restaurants before he returned to Shrewsbury's La Dolce Vita.

Gennaro's parents had moved from Italy to Shrewsbury in 1999 to open the restaurant. The restaurant's enduring success has been driven from day one by two guiding principles. The first was that the customer would always experience the very best food, service, and atmosphere. The second was to expand people's ideas about what Italian food could be beyond pasta and pizza. It isn't just that at La Dolce Vita you get to eat authentic Italian food prepared by an Italian chef in a setting with the feel of a neighbourhood restaurant in Italy (although you do!). It's also that you experience Italian food as fine dining; simultaneously classical and hearty and modern and surprising. Take the 'Surprise Menu', for example. A welcome antidote to the pretension of some tasting menus it invites you to sit back, relax, and trust that Gennaro and the team will take you on a memorable culinary journey.

That everything is made from scratch means long prep lists every morning but there's no other way to create the combinations and depths of tastes and textures that the menu offers. There's a very Mediterranean emphasis on using the finest freshly-prepared ingredients and allowing their flavours to shine through. It isn't about using something for the sake of it. Whether local or imported everything that passes through the kitchens has to be of the best possible quality. So, the freshly-baked bread and meat might be local, for example, but the cheeses are imported from Italy because an Italian restaurant without authentic mozzarella or Parmesan simply isn't an Italian restaurant.

That La Dolce Vita is family-run means that everyone is personally and professionally invested in the success of the restaurant. But given its glowing reviews and growing army of loyal returning customers, it seems like the feeling is mutual!

La Dolce Vita
AGNOLOTTI OF SMOKED POTATO AND ONION

Although made with three 'poor man's' ingredients this deceptively simple dish can be very luxurious when made with smoked potatoes. Over the years, we at La Dolce Vita have had several variations of this recipe on our menu, but this one is a firm family favourite!

Preparation time: 60 minutes | Cooking time: 5-10 minutes | Serves 4-6

Ingredients

For the pasta:

200g OO flour

2 whole eggs, large

25ml olive oil

For the filling:

500g Maris Piper potatoes, peeled and cut into even pieces

Hickory wood chips (for stove top smokers)

50g unsalted butter

200g onion, diced

20ml olive oil

1 sprig of thyme

For the onion petals:

1 medium white onion, peeled

20ml olive oil

For the pickled red onion:

1 medium red onion, peeled, cut into quarter and separate into petals

300ml water

200g sugar

100g white wine vinegar

1 star anise

For the chive oil:

1 bunch of chives

400ml olive oil

For the liquorice sauce:

1 shallot, diced

Garlic, 1 clove, minced

25g unsalted butter

½ stick liquorice root

300ml vegetable stock

200ml double cream

To serve:

50g caramelized sunflower seeds

Sunflower petals, handful

Method

To make the pasta:

Sift the flour and salt through a sieve into a mound and create a well in the centre. Mixing the eggs with the oil, pour into the well and then slowly mix together until a dough forms. Knead for about ten minutes into a tight ball. Wrap this in cling film and rest in the fridge for 30 minutes.

To make the filling:

Placing the potatoes in a pan three-quarters filled with cold water, add a pinch of salt and then bring to the boil. Cook until the potatoes are tender. Drain before lightly smoking the potatoes over the hickory chips in a stove top smoker according to the manufacturer's instructions. The longer they're smoked, the more intense the flavour, so cook according to taste. Then cream the potato, beating in the butter to form a smooth mash before putting to one side. Place the diced onion, oil and thyme into a frying pan and sweat gently until the onion is translucent. Add the mashed potato, blend evenly, and season to taste, before placing the filling in a piping bag. Returning to the dough, roll it out until it's thin enough to see your fingers through it – either through a pasta machine or using a lightly-floured surface. Then, pipe a tube of filling across the pasta sheet, pull the top edge of the pasta over the filling and press lightly to seal. Starting at one end of the parcel, pinch the filling at 2cm intervals to create little parcels and then cut with a pastry wheel to create individual Agnolotti. Put to one side.

To make the onion petals, pickled red onion, chive oil, and liquorice sauce:

Blanch the peeled medium white onion in boiling water for 2 minutes then place into iced water to stop the cooking. Drain and cut the onion in half and then place sliced side down in a pan with the oil over a high heat, allowing it to caramelize before separating into individual petals. Place water, sugar, vinegar and star anise in a pan before bringing to the boil and then pouring over the red onion petals. Place the chives and oil in a blender and blend on full power for 5 minutes or until the oil turns green. Strain through a fine sieve. Add the chopped shallot and garlic to a pan, lightly sweat in the remaining butter before adding the stock and bringing to the boil. Then, add the liquorice stick, infuse for ten minutes before straining and returning to the heat. Adding the cream, bring to a rolling boil, and reduce by roughly one-third. Add seasoning to taste.

To serve:

Cook the Agnolotti in salted boiling water for 3 minutes before draining and lightly glazing with the remaining melted butter. Place in a bowl and garnish with the charred and pickled onion petals, before finishing with the sunflower seeds, petals, and a drizzle of chive oil. Serve immediately.

Where art meets HEART

This popular Shrewsbury venue offers a seasonally-inspired menu, a great atmosphere, and boutique accommodation for the visiting traveller...

If the modern age is all about finding an angle to help you be heard and seen in a world of competing voices, well, The Lion and Pheasant, a restaurant and hotel in Shrewsbury, has them all covered. Take its location for example. One of England's most beautiful historic towns, Shrewsbury is also in the heart of Shropshire, one of Britain's most picturesque counties and it has one of the world's most iconic rivers meandering past. The Lion and Pheasant, then, is ideally placed on the Wyle Cop, a medieval streetscape framed by half-timbered Tudor buildings.

Of course, you can't eat a location. But Shropshire creates some of Britain's finest produce. This is reflected in The Lion and Pheasant's award-winning menu. Harri Alun Williams and his team use the best of what's local to produce hearty food that's full of flavour. The restaurant's à la carte menu showcases seasonal showstoppers, complementing them with a wine-list guaranteed to gladden the hearts of visiting oenophiles. The bar menu, served on Monday to Thursday evenings, takes an eclectic, inventive approach to classic dishes to keep things fresh. Meanwhile for those just passing by, whether needing time-out of a busy modern world or just fancying a change of gears, afternoon tea is also served in the bar and inglenook between Monday and Saturday afternoons from 1-00 until 4-00 pm. Awarded two AA rosettes, all of the menus are constantly updated in order to use the best of what's seasonally available so return visits are very much in order!

Of course, once you have a great location and superb reputation for the food you offer, the final ingredient needed is atmosphere – and again The Lion and Pheasant has it. Guests, diners and those just dropping in for a drink are greeted by a wonderfully welcoming blend of historic quality and sympathetic contemporary design. The clean modern sheen is balanced against wonderfully cosy features like the open log fireplace in the Inglenook bar, the exposed oak beams, and traditionally flagged stone flooring in the dining areas. Run by Jim Littler and staffed by a professional team throughout that never forget to be friendly, it's an approach that's made the Lion and Pheasant a three-star AA hotel – perfect for those looking to relax in luxury after business or pleasure. But it equally excels as a restaurant and bar for those living in or visiting one of Britain's most beautiful towns.

The Lion and Pheasant

The Lion and Pheasant

SIRLOIN OF BEEF WITH GLAZED CHEEK PARCEL AND RICOTTA GNOCCHI WITH WILD GARLIC AND CHERVIL ROOT

This is a wonderful twist on standard beef recipes that takes a classic cut and really peps up the flavours, textures and sophistication level to something extra special.

Preparation time: 15 minutes | Cooking time: 40 minutes | Serves 4

Ingredients

For the sirloin:

600g sirloin

20g dried mushroom

1 banana shallot, chopped

4 cloves garlic, chopped

2 sprigs thyme

Vacuum pack

For the cheek parcel:

4 beef cheeks

1 onion, chopped

1 carrot, chopped

½ leek

4 cloves garlic

2 sprigs thyme

1 litre chicken stock

For the ricotta gnocchi:

250g ricotta cheese

1 egg

70g micro planed Parmesan

60g plain flour

10ml rapeseed

For the chervil root purée:

200g chervil root, peeled

100g cream

2 cloves

1 sprig thyme

Vacuum pack

To serve:

Wild garlic leaves

Method

While it looks like there are a lot of elements to this recipe, it's just a case of planning in advance, starting with the beef cheek, as they take the longest to prep, and bringing things together at the last moment. So, taking the beef cheeks, trim off the sinew. Chop the carrot, onion, and leek. Then, seal the cheeks in a hot pan, and add the vegetables, browning them slightly. Add the chicken stock, braise in a clay pot (or casserole dish) for 8 hours.

With around four hours to go, remove the fat and sinew from the sirloin and then pencil trim it before rolling it in cling-film and placing it in the fridge to set for 3 hours.

Once the beef has cooked, remove it from the oven and pick it down before removing to one side. Strain the remaining stock, place over a medium heat and reduce until it thickens. Then bind the reduced stock and shredded cheek together, using a touch of flour if necessary before seasoning and shaping with a cutter.

With around an hour to go, pan-fry the beef-fat from the sirloin with the dried mushroom, shallot, garlic and thyme. Strain the fat, and put it to one side. Taking the sirloin from the fridge, remove the cling film and vacuum pack with the strained off fat. Heat a pan of water to 52°c, cook the sirloin for 40 minutes.

At the same time, take the ingredients for the chervil root purée, vacuum pack and boil in a pan of water for around 45 minutes.

Towards the end of this time, begin preparing the gnocchi. In a bowl, mix the ricotta, cheese, egg, Parmesan, and rapeseed oil together until evenly blended. Sift in the flour and gently fold. Add seasoning to the mixture. Placing it in a piping bag, pipe this mixture into gnocchi-sized pieces onto a floured surface and roll it out gently. Bringing a pan of salted water to the boil, add a drop of oil and then cook the gnocchi until it floats in the water. Then refresh in ice-cold water.

There are now a lot of elements coming together at the same time, but there is enough time in hand with each to bring them all together for serving. First, remove the sirloin from the vacuum pack and panfry to medium-rare before setting aside to rest. At the same time, place the beef cheek parcel in the oven to warm. Removing the vegetables from the vacuum pack, purée and add seasoning to taste. Then, pan fry the ricotta gnocchi until golden brown alongside 4 wild garlic leaves in an emulsion. Then, plate as seen in the photograph and serve immediately.

The Lion and Pheasant
SWEET PASTRY WITH LEMON CURD AND ITALIAN MERINGUE

The paradox of patisserie is that exactness and precision in the cooking results in sumptuous decadence. The team at the Lion and Pheasant serve up a deliciously rich but light dessert perfect for every occasion.

Preparation time: 40 minutes | Cooking time: 20 minutes | Serves 4

Ingredients

For the sweet pastry:

187g unsalted butter, diced

121g sugar

1 egg, free-range

316g flour, plain

Tart cases

For the lemon curd:

120g lemon juice

3 eggs

150g caster sugar

45g butter

For the Italian meringue:

200g sugar

100g egg whites

Water (enough to just cover the sugar in a pan)

Orange segments

Vanilla ice cream, to serve

Method

Preheat the oven to 200°c, begin by making the sweet pastry. Mix the sugar, flour and diced butter together in a bowl until you have a texture that resembles breadcrumbs. Then, add the egg, binding together to make the dough. Be careful not to overwork this mixture. Wrap this in cling film and chill in the fridge for approximately 30 minutes. Once thoroughly chilled through, line the tart cases and blind bake until they're golden.

Turning your attention to the lemon curd, place the lemon juice and sugar in a pan and raise to a boil. While the heat is coming up, whisk the eggs into soft fluffy peaks. Then, whisk in the boiled lemon juice and sugar before returning to a medium heat and cooking through, whisking constantly. Remove from the heat, adding the butter by whisking it in until it is combined, before pouring into a tub to cool down.

To make the meringue, use a mixing machine on a medium speed. Whisk together 100g of the sugar and egg whites using the machine. Boil the remaining sugar and water together and then pour this mixture into the bowl of the mixing machine until it is combined. Continue whisking until the mixture is thick and glossy and then place in a piping bag.

To serve

Fill the tart cases with the chilled lemon curd to just under the rim. Add 3 orange segments and 1 small scoop of vanilla ice cream to the middle of the tart. Then, pipe the meringue mix around and over the tart, making sure that you cover the ice cream. Then, blow torch the meringue gently (or alternatively place in the preheated oven for 2-3 minutes approximately to colour the meringue). Serve immediately.

Pigging OUT!

Husband and wife team Rob and Fiona Cunningham are marrying old traditions with new opportunities at Maynard's Farm...

The proof of the pudding, we are told, is always in the eating. At Maynard's Farm, they're happy to demonstrate that the same applies to the British porker. Set in a beautiful part of Shropshire, Maynard's offers a traditional farm shop, stuffed with all of the good things that can be done with a pig, alongside local cheeses and pâtés, artisanal chutneys and jams, and staples like fresh eggs, milk and butter. In the meaty heart of the business what's on offer in the shop – and there really is no other way to say it – is the good stuff. You see, Maynard's sells what it makes direct to people who really know good food. A bold claim? Well, The Ritz and The Shard in London, as well as Rick Stein, are all regular customers. Why wouldn't they be? After all, Maynard's Farm creates award-winning produce. Its Treacle-Cured Smoked Streaky Bacon was a Great British Taste Award winner in 2015. It is so good that it had previously been the bacon of choice when chefs Raymond Blanc, Valentine Warner, Fergus Henderson (a man who made his name in pigs), Georgio Locatelli, and Thomasina Miers came together to make their perfect burger for charity Action Against Hunger's 5-star Burger Restaurant challenge at Taste of London 2013. A cause close to Rob and Fiona's hearts, Maynard's Farm returned to support Action Against Hunger's 5-star Haute Dog restaurant for the same charity in 2014.

The commitment to quality is evident across the board. The pork butchery courses the farm runs have been voted one of the top 5 in the country by The Guardian newspaper. Similarly, the private and corporate catering the farm provides, offering bespoke catering for intimate gatherings and artistically presented dining for large numbers too, enjoys a glowing word-of-mouth reputation.

Everything on the farm is fuelled by a drive to connect people to good food. After all, enjoying food starts with an appreciation and respect for its provenance. At Maynard's Farm every link in the chain is visible: the filtches of bacon hanging in the shop can be traced back to the farm's smoke-oven; the sausages are made on-site; while the on-site baker, an alumnus of Rick Stein, uses a wood-fired oven to produce high-quality artisanal bread.

When you add in that the farm also runs beautiful bespoke holiday lets that just happen to be situated in the diverse north of one of Britain's most beautiful counties, well, it's clear that it's worth taking a look at what's going on down on this particular farm!

Maynard's Farm
SLOW ROASTED PORK WITH FENNEL AND LEMON WITH SWEET POTATO AND CORIANDER MASH

This recipe came about when asked to prepare a hog roast for less than 50 people, and is fantastic for a crowd or large party. The flavours are based on an Italian porcetta we discovered in a Tuscan market during a family holiday. It's best to order in advance if you're ordering from Maynard's, or indeed most butchers. A whole shoulder weighing around 8-10 kg will feed around 25 people, so if you do cook for a larger party, simply triple the ingredients below and allow an extra 2 hours cooking from the point when the cider is poured around the meat.

Preparation time: 30 minutes | Cooking time: 3 hours | Serves 8

Ingredients

3-3½ kg of boned pork shoulder, fat well scored

For the spice paste:

2 tsp fennel seeds

1 tsp coriander seeds

1 tsp black peppercorns

1 tsp dried chilli flakes

3 tsp sea salt

4 garlic cloves crushed

1 lemon, zested and juiced

200ml cider

For the sweet potato and coriander mash:

12 medium sweet potatoes

8 unpeeled cloves garlic

Olive oil

1 tsp cinnamon

Sea salt, to taste

Fresh black pepper, to taste

50g butter

Freshly chopped coriander leaves

Sage leaves, to garnish

Method

Preheat the oven to 230°c, crush the fennel, coriander, and peppercorns in a pestle and mortar or grind them in a food processor. Add the chilli, salt, garlic and lemon zest and mix into a paste. Rub the paste into both sides of the meat, pushing it into the fat and scored surfaces, before placing the pork skin side up on a rack in a large roasting pan and drizzling it with olive oil. Popping the pork in the oven, roast it for approximately thirty minutes until the skin begins to sizzle. Remove it from the oven and carefully turn it skin-side down. Pouring over the lemon juice, turn the oven down to 160°c and cook for another hour. At the end of this time, take the pork out of the oven again and turn it skin-side up again before pouring cider around the pork into the roasting dish. Cook at this temperature for a further hour before turning the oven back up to 220°c and letting the fat crisp for a further half an hour.

With ninety minutes to go, place the sweet potatoes on a roasting tray and roast until cooked through. With thirty minutes to go, pop the garlic cloves, drizzled with olive oil, in the oven next to the sweet potatoes.

Once these are cooked through, peel the sweet potatoes and garlic, discarding the skins. Place both in a bowl, add the butter, salt, pepper, cinnamon and some of the coriander before mashing. Keep warm until ready to serve and then drizzle with olive oil and sprinkle with coriander.

Returning to the pork, check its temperature has reached an internal 82°c and garnishing with a handful of sage leaves, place it on a carving board to rest. Skim the fat off the juices before adding a bit more cider and reducing before bringing to the boil. Decant the reduction to a jug to be served alongside the pork.

Serve the pork, mash, and reduction with a green salad or your favourite green vegetables and enjoy!

Moli Tea House
BEIJING DUMPLINGS WITH PORK AND CABBAGE

Based in Shrewsbury's bustling market, Moli Tea house serves authentic Chinese food and tea based on owner Angela Jones's experiences of living in Sichuan, China. It also serves an authentic experience too, with food, spices, teas and decor all echoing what you might find in the back streets of Sichuan – and sourced from authentic outlets. Some of the teas are Sichuan specialities, grown on a sacred mountain in the province.

Preparation time: 30 minutes | Cooking time: 15 minutes | Makes 20

Ingredients

250g minced pork

¼ cabbage, shredded

3 spring onions, chopped

2 inch piece of fresh ginger, grated

4 garlic cloves, crushed

2 tbsp Shaoxing wine

2 tbsp sesame oil

2 tbsp light soy sauce

¼ tsp sugar

Black pepper, one pinch

2 tsp table salt

For the dough:

125g strong white flour

60ml cold water

1 teaspoon vegetable oil to cook

For the dipping sauce:

Light soy sauce

Dark rice vinegar

Chilli oil

Crushed garlic

Sichuan pepper

Sugar

Method

In a bowl, mix the flour and water together and knead for five minutes until smooth. Cover and leave to rest at room temperature for 20 minutes.

Shred the cabbage, sprinkle with salt and set aside for 20 minutes before wringing dry in a tea-towel. Combine the pork mince with the ginger, garlic, Shaoxing wine, sesame oil, soy sauce, sugar and black pepper in a bowl before adding the wrung-out cabbage and chopped spring onions and setting aside.

On an unfloured surface, roll half the dough into a long narrow sausage shape. Then cut into ten pieces and roll each into two inch circles. Repeat with the remaining dough. Spoon 1½ teaspoons of the filling onto the dough circle before folding in half and pinching together in the centre, pleating the edges to create a ribbed crescent shape.

Once you've made the dumplings, heat the vegetable oil in a sauté pan over a medium heat before adding the dumplings. Cook for 2-3 minutes until golden brown on the bottom. Then, pour in enough boiling water to come ⅓ of the way up the dumplings before covering with a lid and cooking for 5-6 minutes (or until the water has been absorbed). Remove the lid and continue cooking the dumplings for 2-3 minutes until they're crisp and dry on the bottom.

Mix the soy sauce and vinegar in a dip bowl before adding the chilli oil, garlic, Sichuan pepper and sugar to taste.

Serve the dumplings and sauce with freshly-made jasmine tea.

Come INN

The local pub used to be the hub of the community. The New Inn at Baschurch keeps that idea very much alive...

Conjure up the image of the ideal village pub in your mind's eye and you'll think of something remarkably similar to The New Inn at Baschurch. Whitewashed outer walls and rustic charm? Check. Roaring log-burners for those cold winter months and a rambling garden for lazy summer days and nights? Check. A wonderful selection of beers, wines, and spirits, including what's best of what's local alongside menus that deliver all of your favourites with fresh, modern twists? Check, check and check.

Hospitality in the form of warm welcomes, good food and the best of what can go in a glass are imprinted into the walls of The New Inn. After all, there's been a public house on the site since 1841. All villages need a pub, and The New Inn is Baschurch's. This picturesque and popular North Shropshire village has Shrewsbury to the South-east, Oswestry to the north-west and Wem to the north-east. But with a history that stretches all the way back to the Norman Conquest it has an identity all of its own and one that The New Inn reflects beautifully.

The building combines the best of its historic features with tastefully understated finishing touches to blend old and new in a manner both inviting and welcoming. Think exposed beams and brickwork with clean modern lines and sophisticated and understated lighting. With its elegant, stylish interiors, and warm, friendly staff it's easy to see why the pub is popular with visitors and guests alike. Part of the appeal is the fact that the food and drink served are excellent. Led by head chef Andrea Birch and overseen by executive chef Chris Conde, like its sister restaurant Henry Tudor House The New Inn's menu takes a passionate and skilful approach to classic staples, such as beer battered haddock and steak and ale pie, and places them alongside tastes of the exotic. The result is a balance of the best local produce and an eclectic way with flavour, each dish complemented by a superbly sourced choice of wines, beers, and spirits.

There are many fine reasons to visit Shropshire. When you do so, there are many equally fine places to call in for sustenance and good cheer. The New Inn is certainly up there with the best of them.

New Inn at Baschurch
RHUBARB AND CUSTARD

This New Inn at Baschurch take on a classic dessert breathes new life into it, if not the classic children's television programme!

Preparation time: 10 minutes | Cooking time: 1 hour | Serves 6

Ingredients

For the panacotta:

600ml cream

150ml milk

150g caster sugar

3 leaves gelatin

Pinch of Saffron

For the rhubarb:

500ml water

200g caster sugar

2 sticks of rhubarb

1 vanilla pod

100ml grenadine

For the meringue:

150g egg whites

110g caster sugar

For the honeycomb:

160g caster sugar

80g golden syrup

2 tsp bicarbonate of soda

For the jelly:

Reserved poaching liquor

5 leaves gelatin

Method

Begin by preparing the meringues, as they'll take the longest. Preheat the oven to 100°c, whisk the egg whites into soft peaks, gradually adding in the caster sugar. Place the mixture into a piping bag before piping small peaks of mixture onto a sheet of baking paper. Then, bake for 1 hour or until the meringues come away from the baking sheet without leaving any residue.

To make the Panna cotta, first soak the gelatine in cold water until it blooms. Add the rest of the ingredients into a pan and bring it to the boil. Squeeze the gelatin to rid it of any excess water, and then whisk into the cream mixture in the pan before allowing to cool slightly and then pouring into glasses.

To prepare the rhubarb, put the water, sugar, grenadine and scraped vanilla pod into a pan and then bring it to the boil. Peeling the rhubarb and cutting it into 2cm pieces add it to the pan and poach it until it is al dente before removing and putting it aside. Keep the poaching liquor however as you will need it to make the jelly.

For the jelly

Place five leaves of gelatine into cold water to bloom. Warm the poaching liquor and then add the gelatin, making sure that any excess water has been squeezed off. Then allow to cool to room temperature while making the honeycomb.

To make the honeycomb

add the caster sugar and syrup into a pan and heat until amber in colour (on a sugar thermometer the temperature should be around 150°c). At this temperature, whisk in the bicarbonate of soda and pour it onto a baking sheet before allowing it to cool before breaking it into pieces.

To serve

When the Panna cotta has set, pour over the jelly to a depth of 5mm. Allow the jelly to set in a fridge before adding three sticks of poached rhubarb, meringue, and the broken pieces of honeycomb.

A jewel in the
CROWN

Luxurious elegance, fine dining and a fine location mean that Old Downton Lodge should be a tick on any visitor's list of places to visit in Shropshire...

Anyone turning these pages will sooner rather than later have to come to the conclusion that Shropshire is more studded with foodie gems and culinary jewels than a royal tiara. This is a county that doesn't just 'do' food – it loves it, and it does it exceptionally well. But even among Shropshire's glittering prizes Old Downton Lodge stands out. A restaurant with rooms, the Lodge is a 3 AA rosette-winning and Michelin-listed establishment whose 10 luxury bedrooms are set amongst medieval, half-timbered buildings that date back to the Georgian period. There's a modern sensibility to the finish, though, so guests are offered the best form of pure escapism: historic character, modern luxury, and a memorable fine-dining experience in a secluded rural setting whose views of the Hereford and Shropshire hills are nothing short of spectacular. This is, after all, a place that has won an 'Editor's Choice' at the Good Hotel Guide 2016 award; a place where diners, guests at the hotel, and reception and conference attendees can relax into its immersive atmosphere.

The award-winning prowess doesn't stop there, either, but continues through to the kitchen, headed by Karl Martin. There is a tasting menu served from Tuesday and Saturday nights that changes every day. Served in a dining room reputed to date back to the Norman Conquest and capable of holding thirty people for a formal occasion or becoming intimate when set for tables of two or four, the six course and nine course tasting menus make the most of Shropshire's fantastic local produce. It can be as simple as Monkfish with pork, beetroot and apple followed by Venison with artichoke, walnuts, blue cheese and pear. But even in these enlightened days it's a rare place with the confidence and craft to trust the flavours of the produce to come through. It speaks volumes about Shropshire, and volumes about Old Downton Lodge's approach to food.

The wine-list is equally spectacular. Designed by Alexios Stasinopoulos to complement and transcend the food and supplied by Tanner's, an independent Shropshire wine merchant since 1842, the Lodge has over 165 different wines in the cellars, 26 of which are served by the glass. These are wines you can enjoy with your meal, or while watching the sun set from the courtyard. Factor in that the whole lodge is available for exclusive use, meaning that it's available for intimate parties to get away from it all, and whether for personal peace and quiet or corporate events Old Downton Lodge is practically perfect in every way!

Old Downton Lodge

Old Downton Lodge
PORK WITH ONION, MUSHROOM AND MISO

Using the Kobe beef of the pork world, Old Downton Lodge serves up a tasty combination of textures and flavours in this sophisticated but surprisingly easy to make dish.

Preparation time: 36 hours | Cooking time: 45 minutes to 1 hour | Serves 4

Ingredients

For the pork:

2 mangalitsa pork tender loins

250g mangalitsa pork belly

100g salt

100g sugar

For the mushroom purée:

300g button mushrooms

50g butter

For the miso caramel:

200g miso

80g sugar

160g water

For the onions:

4 small brown skin onions

Oil

For the picked shitake mushrooms:

50g shitake mushrooms

100g water

100g white wine vinegar

50g sugar

For the garnish:

Mushroom powder

Yarrow

Method

To prepare the belly, cover it with the salt and sugar and place it in the fridge for 24 hours. Then, rinse the belly well under cold water and dry. Place the belly in a vacuum pac bag and cook it in a water bath for 2 days at 65˚c. Then, remove, and place it in the fridge with a heavy tray placed on top of it to press it down.

Then, prepare the fillet. Trim the sinew away from the fillet before placing it in vacuum pac and cooking in a water bath for 40 minutes at 60˚c.

While this is cooking, prepare the other elements. To make the mushroom purée, melt the butter in a pan on a low heat and then add the mushrooms. When the mushrooms are cooked through, add a drop of water and then blitz to a smooth purée in a blender. Sieve through, and season to taste.

To prepare the onions cut, them lengthways, leaving the skins on, and then place them flat side down into a preheated pan with a small amount of oil. Cook until golden brown and then finish under the grill on its lowest setting until they're soft. Then, put them to one side.

To make the picked shitakes, first wash them well in cold water. Place the rest of the ingredients in a pan and then bring it to the boil before adding the mushrooms. Then, remove from the heat, cover, and allow it to cool. This will cook the mushrooms through.

To make the miso caramel, add half of the water to the sugar and place both over a medium heat. Then, raise the temperature of the mixture to 120˚c, whisking to make sure it doesn't stick. Remove from the heat to add the miso and then place back on the heat, whisking constantly. Once these elements are combined, add the rest of the water, and allow to cool.

To serve

Place the pork loin back in the water bath at 60˚c for 15 minutes to reheat. While it's warming, cut the pork belly into slices and then remove the skin from the onions and warm under the grill on a low temperature. Draining the shitake mushrooms from the pickling liquor, place them to one side. Taking a plate, spoon the miso caramel onto it. Putting the loin and belly into a hot pan, seal until golden brown before cutting the loin into slices. Arrange both cuts on the plate. Add the pickled shitakes and onions in and around the pork, and then dot the mushroom purée around the plate. Finish with a garnish of yarrow and mushroom powder and serve immediately.

Originals of THE SPECIES

A ground-zero launch pad for the next generation of chefs, Origins serves up high-class food alongside its programmes of study.

At its best, education should simultaneously be a process of receiving or giving systematic instruction and an enlightening experience. Origins, Shrewsbury College's award-winning commercially run and licensed restaurant and a centre of educational excellence, goes beyond just ticking those boxes though.

It isn't just that visiting customers get to enjoy exceptional food and service in a warm, welcoming environment – although if the glowing reviews are anything to go by they almost certainly do. Nor is it simply that the college's students get to learn from qualified and experienced chefs and front-of-house staff about every aspect of the food industry from creating a complementary and balanced menu to providing a wonderful customer experience – although they do. It isn't solely that the restaurant, the college, and the students work with the best local producers and food professionals; or that the teaching staff gets to pass on their knowledge to the next generation – although they all do too.

It's more that all of this happens all of the time at Origins. It's the sort of experience where everyone wins. Its education as

it should be, but sometimes isn't. Yes, the restaurant provides training for a future career and pathways into industry – the current buzzwords in educational programmes. But it also opens eyes and helps people to achieve things that they didn't think or know that they could. It inspires, motivates, and enthuses even as teaches –far older and more worthy definitions of the purpose of education.

'Our students are classically trained,' explains Steve, one of the lecturers running Origins. 'But we incorporate all of the elements of modern cooking approaches.' On top of that, regular Master-classes with local luminaries mean that students have a rounded experience. They get to put this into practice too, and not just daily in the restaurant itself. Origins and its students are a familiar presence for those visiting the Shrewsbury Food Festival, a 200-stall jamboree of top chefs and live music where a great time is had by all.

Factor in that the restaurant and thus the work of the students is open to the public, features an ever-changing menu that showcases the very best of what Shropshire has to offer and it really is a case of top marks all 'round!

Origins

Origins

DUCK COOKED THREE WAYS WITH SMOKED PEAR

A hearty modern spin on an underused game bird results in a luscious feast of tastes and textures.

Preparation time: 60 minutes | Cooking time: 3 hours | Serves 4

Ingredients

1 whole duck (heart and liver to be used)

100g onion

3 bulbs garlic

200g carrot

3 sticks celery

2 bay leaves

10g black peppercorns

4 sprigs of thyme

100ml Port

Goose fat

300g celeriac

100g butter

100ml whipping cream

100ml milk

1 pear

2 baby carrots

2 baby turnips

2 round shallot

200g spinach

50g pea shoots

1 sprig of parsley

Olive oil

Egg

Salt and pepper

Method

The heart and livers need to be trimmed of all fat and gristle. Dust them in seasoned flour. Then dip in egg wash followed by coating in breadcrumbs. Place in fridge until needed.

To prepare the duck

Preheat the oven to 170-180°c, begin by filleting the duck into portions, separating into legs, breasts, and carcass. Then, place the carcass into a roasting tray with the celery, onion, carrots and garlic before roasting it until golden brown. This will take approximately 20-30 minutes per pound of duck. Then, place the roast duck and vegetables in a pan of water, add the peppercorns thyme, and bay leaves and bring to the boil before reducing the heat and simmering for 2-4 hours, skimming throughout. Once this is underway, reduce the heat of the oven to 140°c. Place the legs into the roasting tray, coat liberally with goose fat and then confit cook in the oven for approximately two hours, or until tender. Remove them from the oven, wait for them to cool before picking the meat off the bone, and adding the chopped parsley, salt and pepper mix together in a bowl. Rolling the mixture in cling-film to resemble a sausage place it in the fridge to set. Taking one of the duck breasts, vacuum pack it with butter and thyme. Place this in a water bath at 55°c for an hour and a half.

To make the vegetables

Dice the celeriac and place into a pan. Add the milk and cream and simmer until tender. Removing the pan from the heat, add the butter and then purée together into a smooth mixture before seasoning to taste with salt and pepper and straining the mixture through a sieve. Filling a pan with water, bring it to the boil before adding the baby carrots and turnips. After two minutes of a rolling boil, remove from the heat, drain, and place the vegetables into cold water to refresh. Rub to remove the outside skin. Bringing another pan of water to the boil, add the shallots. After two minutes, remove from the heat and drain. Char-grill and then roast the shallots until they darkened in colour

To make the smoked pear

Dice the pear into 1 x 1 cm cubes, then place in a wood chip smoker for 20 minutes to smoke the pear. Alternatively, brush the pear pieces with colgin liquid smoke and bake in the oven for 5 minutes

To serve

Returning to the duck stock, strain it and then reduce it by heating by three-quarters before adding the port. Returning to the final duck breast, take a heavy-bottom pan and place the breast skin-side down. Bringing up to heat, seal all sides of the breast until there is an internal temperature of 55°c. Deep or shallow fry the bread crumbed offal (heart/livers) until golden brown, cut in half and present on plate.

At the last moment, melt some butter in a pan until foaming, add the spinach for 20 seconds, season and place on a paper towel. Arrange as seen, and serve immediately.

Modern CLASSICS!

At Restaurant Severn, the team have brought together their expertise to deliver all that's great and good in contemporary cuisine.

There must be something in the air and water in Shropshire. After decades in the doldrums, Britain shed its international reputation as a culinary desert a while ago. We're more informed about food now than we've ever been. Across the country, we eat better and we have more choice now than we have ever had. But it's still noteworthy that the place which competes most successfully with London as a food mecca is this small county in the west of the country. Restaurant Severn brings all of the elements that make Shropshire special under one award-winning roof: the best local produce delivered to consistently high-standards in a fresh contemporary style by people who are passionate about food.

Facing Abraham Darby's world-heritage cast iron bridge, with a contemporary interior, bare wooden floors and tables and quirky light fittings Restaurant Severn offers something of a brassiere feel to visitors. But its intimate style belies the fine dining on offer. Open for lunch and dinner from Wednesday to Sunday, the menus are a combination of updated British classics and interpretations of the best that our continental cousins have to offer. As with so many Shropshire eateries, the emphasis is on local produce. But when produce this good is on your doorstep why wouldn't it be? There's a lovely focus on seasonality that's reflected in classical dishes such as the crisp hen's egg with buttered asparagus spears, but the British countryside peeks through in the flavour combinations. For example, the treacle cured fillet of beef is finished with a Port jelly and red wine jus for a distinctive series of complementary flavour combinations. Those with vegan and gluten-free requirements can also be accommodated with a little advance notice too. There's a quality and thoughtfulness to the lunch and dinner menus that illustrates the passion and craft that the team use to bring an incredible dining experience to the table. It's this that's led to Restaurant Severn's double AA-rosettes for culinary excellence. But while it can do formal exceptionally well, it's also a perfect venue to pop along to and unwind with a glass of wine, confident in the knowledge that a fantastic meal is on its way to you. Definitely one to visit!

Restaurant Severn

TREACLE-CURED BEEF, CHATEAU POTATOES, BRAISED SHALLOTS AND CHESTNUT MUSHROOMS

A dish inspired by our chef's hero Tom Kerridge, here at Restaurant Severn we cook the beef in a water bath at a low temperature, but you'll get equally excellent results at home using your oven – which is the method we've recommended here!

Preparation time: 8 hours (for the marinade) | Cooking time: 1 hour | Serves 4

Ingredients

4 fillets of beef (150g each, approx)

50g treacle

50ml water

Salt and pepper

8 medium-sized floury potatoes (Maris piper, for example)

75ml port

25ml red wine

25ml red wine vinegar

1 gelatine leaf

8 chestnut mushrooms, quartered

150g butter

10ml truffle oil

25g caster sugar

3 banana shallots, peeled and halved

50ml vegetable stock

200g butternut squash, diced

250ml beef stock

100g redcurrant jelly

250ml red wine

Salt and pepper

Method

Marinate the beef by mixing the treacle and water and place all three in a container overnight or for 8 hours. Turn occasionally to ensure evenness. Then, remove the beef from the marinade and pat dry before adding the marinade to a pan and gently reduce by half. Season with salt and pepper.

Preheat the oven to 55°c (or your lowest possible setting). Then, heating a little oil in a large pan over a high heat, add a knob of butter, and fry the beef all over. Place the beef in a roasting tin and transfer it to the bottom shelf off the oven for 60 minutes.

While this is roasting, turn your attention to the other elements of the dish.

Preheat a second oven to 200°c and bring a large pan of salted water to the boil. Add the potatoes and cook until soft on the outside. Drain and then cool on a wire rack. Add a little oil to a roasting tin and place in the oven to heat. Add the potatoes, stirring gently to make sure they're evenly coated in oil and roast for 40 minutes until they're crisp and brown.

While they're roasting, make the Port jelly by bringing all of the port, red wine and red wine vinegar to the boil in a saucepan before reducing it to a simmer for 15 minutes to ensure the vinegar is cooked off. Meanwhile, put the gelatine leaf in a bowl with a little cold water. Once it has softened, add the mixture from the pan and dissolve. Set aside, and cut into squares once cooled.

Prepare the mushrooms by heating them with 50g of the butter and truffle oil in a frying pan, keeping them moving to make sure the mushrooms colour nicely. Season.

Cook off the shallots in vegetable stock for 5 minutes until soft. Remove and cut in half once they've cooled, retain the stock for the squah. Then, add them and add 50g of butter to the frying pan, cooking them cut side down for 2 minutes until they're caramelised. Then remove from the pan. Prepare the squash by heating in a pan with the rest of the butter and retained vegetable stock until soft, then drain and purée with a hand-blender and pass through a sieve.

Remove the beef, brush with the remaining marinade and leave to rest.

Prepare the red wine jus by bringing the beef stock, redcurrant jelly and red wine to the boil together in a pan and simmer until thickened.

To serve

Put a tablespoon of purée on a plate, add the potatoes, mushrooms, and the beef, before placing the shallots on the top and drizzling all over with the red wine jus.

The Riverside at AYMESTREY

As in every walk of life, fashions in food change too. But regardless of fads and trends at the heart of all great food lies a simple premise: you're only as good as your ingredients. Local produce is currently a foodie buzzword. In an age where carbon footprints and air miles have entered everyday language, the idea is that superb ingredients and produce can be found on one's doorstep rather than on the other side of the world. Shropshire is lucky in that regard as some of the finest produce in Britain is created within its borders.

The Riverside at Aymestrey takes the concept of 'local' one step further with its 'seed to plate' ethos. The idea is that the provenance of every element on the menu can be traced. The vegetables and herbs are drawn from the garden, for example. With its own bee-hives, in 2016 the orchards were significantly extended and perennial crops introduced to serve the kitchen's needs better. The gardens are open too, with the team happy to show guests and diners around. Local is one thing, but to be able to see where what you're going to eat has been nurtured and grown is quite another! On a daily basis, the team forage in the nearby meadows, hedgerows, and riverbanks for wild garlic, elderflower, nettles and more to add to the pot. Similarly meat and other ingredients are sourced to the level of the farm and the producer, drawing in the best of what North Herefordshire, the Welsh Borders, and South Shropshire's farms have to offer.

"Each dish has a story," explains Andy, now chef patron and owner after previously working at The Riverside as head chef for a decade. 'And every item on the menu is there for a reason.'

The flavours on offer are inspired by classic British flavours. Betraying modern influences, they're served in a country style that might best be described as elegantly rustic. Everything is cooked freshly on-site. This really is a dining experience that immerses you in the local landscape.

And what a landscape it is. Although it remains handy for Ludlow and Hereford, the sixteenth-century timber-framed inn is folded deep into the countryside on the southern edge of Mortimer Forest with the river Lugg running through the grounds – and fishing rights available for guests. With five golf courses, the Black and White Village Trail, Ludlow, Hereford, numerous heritage sites, breweries, cider presses, cheese-wrights, visitor centres and country parks all within striking distance The Riverside makes a superb base for the adventurous. Or you could just take a walk in the gardens, decide what you want for lunch, and then relax, safe in the knowledge that a superb meal is on its way...

The Rosette Award for Culinary Excellence 2016 - 2017

Riverside
HAY-BAKED SHROPSHIRE GUINEA FOWL WITH CARROT, BARLEY AND HERBS

Sometimes the best dishes come from our childhood memories. Growing up, we often kept poultry on hay, feeding them everything from vegetable trimmings to different grains. From this, we created a dish based around pairing grains and guinea fowl incorporating vegetables and herbs grown by myself and my team of chefs.

Preparation time: 7 minutes | Cooking time: 20-30 minutes | Serves 2

Ingredients

Guinea fowl or chicken bones (ask your local butcher for these)

2 onions, chopped

4 cloves garlic, chopped

3 sticks celery, chopped

3 mushrooms, chopped

80g malt grains or toasted barley

Thyme, 2 sprigs

Rosemary, 2 sprigs

3–4 bay leaves

1 tbsp malt extract

60g rolled toasted wheat flakes

2 tbsp honey (we used honey from own hive)

2 guinea fowl breasts

4 tbsp Bennett & Dunn Rapeseed Oil

4 tbsp Butter

Dried hay, small handful

6-8 organic or home-grown carrots

40g butter

15ml hazelnut oil

Wild herbs, a selection (we use yarrow, hairy bitter cress, and dandelion leaves in this recipe)

Method

To make the broth:

Preheat the oven to 180°c. Placing them in a roasting pan, roast the guinea fowl or chicken bones for 1 hour. Over a medium heat, fry the chopped onion and three-quarters of the garlic, mushroom, and celery until they are brown before adding the barley and frying off. Then, add the roasted bones, and half of the thyme, rosemary and bay leaves before covering with water. Simmer this for 6 hours until it is light brown in colour and has a good flavour. Then, sieve into a second pan and reduce by half, adding the malt extract. Taste and season accordingly.

To make the wheat flakes:

Lightly fry off the remaining garlic in a splash of rapeseed oil and a knob of butter, adding the remaining thyme and rosemary. Add the rolled wheat flakes and honey. Roast these until golden, blending and seasoning to taste.

To make the guinea fowl:

Preheat the oven to 190°c, fry the guinea fowl breasts in an oven-proof pan in a splash of oil, making sure that they are sealed on all sides. Then, add the butter and position the hay around it. Igniting the hay, cover with foil before placing the pan in the oven and roasting for 12-15 minutes. Smoking in this manner can be difficult at home (especially where smoke alarms are involved!). Stove top smokers are available. Alternatively, use an outside BBQ for a few minutes before using the oven to finish.

To make the carrot purée

Peel the carrots, chop them, and place them in a pan and cover them with water. Cook them until they are soft (approx 10-15 minutes), and then drain. Mash with the butter and hazelnut oil until they are smoothly blended, then season to taste. Put to one side.

To serve:

Spoon the carrot purée onto a plate. Slice the guinea fowl and place in the centre. Tossing the foraged herbs in the warm meat juices, add these to the plate before sprinkling over the toasted wheat crumb. Serve with the sauce.

Market FORCES!

Shrewsbury Market Hall is a slice of living history, a communal hub, a foodie paradise and a jolly good day out...

In many ways, Shrewsbury's Market Hall sums up Shrewsbury. That there's a market here at all is a nod to Shrewsbury's status as a market town. There's been one in Shrewsbury since the late-thirteenth century; a historic marker of Shrewsbury's status as the commercial and communal hub of Shropshire. It's a status that endures to this day. The current version of the Market Hall was opened with pomp, ceremony and pageantry in 1965. To some, these were the decades that civic architecture forgot, as a brutalist style swept out many historic buildings and replaced them with concrete confections that won plaudits and brickbats in equal measure. But enough time has passed for The Market Hall to stand alongside Shrewsbury's 660 listed buildings as a reminder of the town's illustrious history. Now, as then, the market brings together everything good about Shrewsbury and Shropshire under one roof.

The market has undergone a renaissance in recent years, driven by inventive independent businesses who have embraced growing awareness of the importance of 'real' food and the fantastic array of artisan producers and local produce that Shrewsbury has on its doorstep. The market is rightly a magnet for foodies, a must-visit destination boasting some of the most creative lunch spots that Shrewsbury has to offer. They're augmented by stalls populated with artisan food producers and those selling fresh local produce drawn from Shropshire's fantastically fertile landscape. It says a lot that some of these have been trading for over half a century and more. For those looking to mooch and browse, it's also worth noting the string of contemporary lifestyle, home accessory and gift boutiques, vintage stalls, art and crafts studios, vinyl records, secondhand books, bikes and much more.

All of these help to make the market the attraction that it is, but it's food we're concerned with here, and the market certainly delivers!

Let's start with the House of Yum, described by The Guardian newspaper as vying with the Bird's Nest Cafe, another Market Hall favourite, as the 'best lunch spot' in town. Specialising in Thai street food, this quirky café cooks everything from scratch, sourcing many of their ingredients within the market. This is a common theme within the market, but the relationship between Barkworths Seafoods and St. Pierre Bar, featured elsewhere in this book, is closer still. The latter grew from the former, when owner Ian Cornall's experiment in selling Champagne and oysters on the stall was such a success that it blossomed into St. Pierre's, the sort of continental-style seafood bar that gives fresh fish and freshly-prepared dishes such a good name.

Shrewsbury Market Hall

The idea of places you can drop into on the hoof is another recurring theme of the market. Take Indian Street Food Takeaway, Café AleOli, Moli Tea House, and The Market Buffet café. They're each very different, but all have one thing in common: great food, freshly prepared. Indian Street Food serves curries to take away fresh from bubbling pans. Café AleOli sees owner Frances O'Shea serving up her passion for Spain in freshly-made tapas dishes and occasional sell-out flamenco evenings that bring Iberian culture to Shrewsbury. Meanwhile, Angela Jones' Moli Tea House offers authentically made Chinese pork dumplings and real Chinese tea. Both of these cafes are featured in this book and it is well worth checking out their fantastically tasty recipes as well as paying them a visit in person. Also worthy of a mention, is The Market Buffet Café, run by members of the same family for 49 years! It's been a stopping-point for generations of Salopians, and is justly famed for its homebaked pies, quiches, pastries and cakes. For those in touch with their inner hip young thing (and those who just like great food) the Bird's Nest Café is a must-visit. Run by young chefs with an unerring focus on high-quality locally-sourced ingredients it serves a tasty menu under a nest of willow branches woven into a canopy of fairy lights. It was recently voted Shropshire's Best Independent Coffee Shop/Café.

The market also has a wealth of stalls that sell all you need to conjure up your own food magic. Delicatessen Cook and Carve has been trading for three decades and offers a counter packed with artisan cheeses, cooked meats and their own cured bacon. There are also four separate family butchers including WD Dodd, focussing on traditional breeds, and Corbett's, a poultry and game specialist. All use traditional methods of hanging meat to produce flavour and source from local farms and suppliers. Meanwhile Snapdragon Wholefoods is a destination for organic and fair-trade produce such as grains, pulses, rice, pasta, dried fruits, nuts and rapeseed oils. It stocks over 100 herbs and spices, 60 different teas, 30 different flours as well as a vast range of fairtrade chocolate. For the gourmands new venture Black Box create their own spice blends for stews, marinades and barbecue rubs. Fruit and vegetable stalls abound with Hopesay Glebe Farm offering organic produce.

And no good meal is complete, of course, without the perfect complementing drink. Iron and Rose, established by Robin Nugent after twenty years in the wine industry, handpick their wines from small production vineyards that use only natural, ethical and authentic methods of production. They're wines, he says that "speak of the people and the places that made them, filled with life and individuality". It's a mantra that could well sum up all that is best about Shrewsbury Market Hall.

Shrewsbury Market Hall

The word on
THE STREET

Going the whole hog and much, much more, Smoked Shropshire is going from strength to strength as it brings smoky flavours to its street-food menus...

Life-skills coaching suggests that our passions are what drive us and that if we can turn our hobbies into our day jobs, we will flourish. A great example of this is Smoked Shropshire, a thriving family business that has evolved out of the hobbies of not one but three members of the Williams family; Ben and his parents Ruth and Andy.

For a while, Ben was in Bedfordshire teaching and managing the school farm. Alongside developing a charcuterie and catering enterprise to keep the farm afloat financially, he was also producing rare-breed livestock for Michelin-starred restaurants in London. Back home at their Pool Cottage Smallholding in Shropshire, Ruth and Andy were busy raising livestock and turning their produce into a variety of culinary and charcuterie delights. But, as in all of the best enterprises, the final piece of the jigsaw fell into place following a chance meeting that led to Ben and Andy competing at Meatopia, a major London festival of high-quality, ethically sourced meat, cooked over ethically sourced wood and charcoal by some of the world's leading chefs. Realising that if they could hold their own in such company then their 'living the dream' motto could become a reality; Ben found his way back home and Smoked Shropshire was born.

Part of the increasingly popular street food scene, Smoked Shropshire specialises in low n' slow cooking using only the very best local produce, home reared by the family and friends. The meltingly tender 12-hour smoked mutton and beef brisket, delicious pulled pork and flavoursome ribs are is complimented by fresh salads, salsas and slaws. The bacon is home-cured to ensure flavour and texture are just right, and the Smoked Shropshire team produce all the charcuterie they serve. Street-food's ethos is to share and Smoked Shropshire's love is spread out to the customers not only through the food, but also on the courses that the team offer in smoking, curing, sausage-making, cider production and other smallholder activities.

Smoked Shropshire operates at local food events, and also offers private catering options for weddings, birthdays and other special celebratory events. The most popular product is the slow-cooked mutton. As with all the meats, it's seasoned and then cooked over live fire with wood and charcoal to give an amazing depth of flavour. When this approach is taken with slow-grown, high-welfare produce like mutton, well, then you're in the realm of foodie heaven. Pair this up with fresh citrus and world-food flavours (rather than sticky sauces and creamy coleslaws) and you're looking at food made with love that's really ticking all of the right boxes. Smoked Shropshire's offering is definitely one to try.

LOW 'N' SLOW

Smoked

MADE IN SHROPSHIRE

Smoked Shropshire
SMOKED MUTTON WITH COCONUT DAHL AND MANGO SALSA

This recipe takes a little time but it's worth it for the flavours the cooking process unlocks.

Preparation time: 1 hour | Cooking time: 13 hours | Serves 4

Ingredients

1 shoulder of mutton (3–4kg)

2tbsp cumin

1 onion, diced

Cooking oil (we use local rapeseed oil)

2 garlic cloves, crushed

2 red chillies, diced

4cm ginger root, grated

1tsp turmeric

250g of white lentils

800ml chicken stock

400ml coconut milk

6 curry leaves

Saffron, a generous pinch

Coriander, 1 bunch

1 lime, juiced

1 mango, diced (1cm cubes)

Salt and pepper, to taste

Method

The first thing to do is to prepare the smoker or BBQ (with a lid) for indirect cooking. Place coals in one half of the BBQ and a pan of water next to them. Light the coals and allow the BBQ to reach 130˚c.

Place some lumps of hardwood such as oak into the hot coals. Rub the mutton all over with cumin and then place it on the side of the smoker or BBQ opposite the coals. Smoke uncovered for 3-4 hrs before placing in a roasting tray, seal with tin foil and continue smoking for a further 8-9 hours before allowing the meat to rest for 30 minutes.

If you don't have a smoker and want to use the oven instead, place some onion halves in a roasting tray. Rub the mutton all over with the cumin and then lay it on top of the onion, adding enough water to cover the bottom to a depth of 1cm. Then cover tightly with foil and cook at 160˚c for at least 6 hours.

With about an hour to go with either method, make the dahl. Dicing the onion, sauté it in a little oil over a low heat until it turns translucent. Add the garlic, one of the diced chillies and the ginger allowing these to soften before adding the turmeric. Stir for 1 minute before adding the lentils, stirring again to coat the lentils in the spices.

Then, add the stock, coconut milk, curry leaves and saffron, seasoning with salt and pepper before allowing it to simmer for an hour. Stir it at least every 10 minutes and then more often in the last 10-15 minutes as the mixture thickens. If you feel it is thickening too much, add a drop more water to make sure that you end with a consistency close to a pasta sauce.

Finally, to make the salsa, chop the coriander and add the remaining chilli, lime juice and the diced mango together in a bowl, stirring well to combine.

To serve

Pulling the mutton off the shoulder, serve on a plate with a generous portion of dahl topped with mango salsa. It's also a dish that goes superbly with fresh flat breads or naan.

A bird of a different FEATHER

Telford's The Ugly Duckling takes traditional ingredients for success and turns them into something new...

The saying is that if you don't have a go, you'll die wondering. Take Thomas Telford's Grade-I listed cast-iron bridge. Located just a couple of miles up the road from The Ugly Duckling at Longdon-on-Tern it took a man with a plan to bring it into existence. Similarly, it took two friends from Telford and their sons to conjure The Ugly Duckling out of thin air. It didn't matter that they had little background in restaurants beyond enjoying eating and drinking in them or little grounding in food and drink beyond knowing what was good when they tasted it. Spotting an opportunity, with careful planning, a willingness to learn, a lot of hard work, and a fantastic team they've turned an old Punch Tavern on the outskirts of Telford into a vibrant, fresh example of all that's best in food and drink.

'When you start from scratch the team is the most important thing,' explains Mitch. 'From Will in the kitchen to my Dad taking on the renovation and building work we all pull together. What we wanted to create was not just a place where other people would want to eat, but the sort of place where we would want to eat too.'

Their motto is better than pub grub. That doesn't mean that pub classics are absent from the menu, but they're given a

fresh, modern twist. They're also placed alongside an à la carte menu and an approach to programming that means that The Ugly Duckling appeals across the board to customers who have grown savvy about their food. If you fancy a steak with all the trimmings, well, the very best local beef cooked over charcoal to lock the flavours in is on offer. But options like 'Fish and Fizz' on a Friday give a new spin to traditional pre-weekend provender while grazing menus mean that you don't have to be tied in to a full sit down meal. You can just come in for a drink, sit down, relax, and catch up with friends or family. Each menu changes regularly to reflect the very best available produce too.

A simultaneous commitment to providing both the high-quality experience in and out of the kitchen and the flexibility and choice customers now want seems an obvious recipe for success. Simple recipes, however, are often the hardest to pull off. However, if the five-star recommendations, bubbling word-of-mouth, and full tables are anything to go by, then it's a recipe that The Ugly Duckling cooks to perfection.

The Ugly Duckling
STICKY TOFFEE PUDDING WITH CLOTTED CREAM AND SALTED TOFFEE SAUCE

This simple recipe takes a novel twist on an established stick-to-your-ribs winter classic for a filling dessert.

Preparation time: 15 minutes | Cooking time: 20 minutes | Serves 10

Ingredients

For the pudding:

250g dates

6g bicarbonate-of-soda

375ml boiling water

80g beef suet

125g dark brown sugar

125g light soft brown sugar

2 free-range eggs

325g Self-raising flour

6g baking powder

Salt, a pinch

Bennett and Dunn rapeseed oil

Plain flour, for dusting

For the salted toffee sauce:

250g unsalted butter

250g dark brown sugar

250g double cream

Maldon salt, pinch

For the garnish:

Good quality clotted cream

Fresh garden mint

Method

To make the toffee pudding

Soak the dates in boiling water and the bicarbonate-of-soda and then leave it for 15 minutes. In a large bowl, mix the suet and sugar together and then add the eggs before blending in the flour, salt and baking powder. Then, blitz the dates and the water together in a food processor before adding it to the flour mixture and mixing well.

Preheat the oven to 180°c, lightly grease 10 large dariol moulds with Bennett and Dunn rapeseed oil and plain flour, half-fill the moulds with batter and then place foil over the top of each one. Placing some old newspaper in the bottom of a baking tray, put the moulds on top and fill the baking tray with boiling water to half way up the moulds. Carefully place these in the oven and bake for 18-22 minutes approximately.

To make the salted toffee sauce

Dice the butter into a pan, add the sugar and cream, and then put on a low heat until dissolved. Once dissolved, turn up the heat and bring the pan to the boil for 30 seconds. Remove from the heat and then add a large pinch of Maldon salt and mix together.

To serve:

Place a sticky toffee pudding in the centre of a plate and drizzle the toffee sauce over it before topping with fresh mint and clotted cream.

Thinking PIG

Peter and Alison Themans are making the most of one of Shropshire's prime resources...

You could only find Wenlock Edge Farm Shop, an enduring labour of love for Peter and Alison Themans, in Shropshire. Shropshire is, after all, the county of one of P.G. Wodehouse's most enduring creations, the residence and inhabitants of Blandings Castle – a place where the sun always shines and the adventures are always madcap, but as far as Lord Emsworth is concerned all that matters is his prize pig the Empress of Blandings. Think Shropshire, then, and you think pig – a philosophy that's at the heart of what's happening down on this particular farm.

You see, Wenlock Edge Farm specialises in the art of curing bacon and producing artisan pork products in a way that's all but been lost: the traditional way. It's an approach that works too. Each week, Wenlock makes at least ten different varieties of sausages, as well as a range of bacons and hams, and a selection of air-dried products like chorizo, salami, prosciutto, pancetta and coppa. The bacon and hams are prize-winning, with their numerous accolades and gold awards marking them among the very best in the country. The Muscovado-cured back bacon has won Best Fresh Product at the Great Taste Awards, for example, making it officially the best-tasting bacon in Britain. Wenlock Farm Products have also won the

prestigious Heart of England Fine Foods diamond award. The sausages too are award-winning, but what marks them out as something special is the fact that so many customers and critics have described them as 'proper sausages' that the name has stuck and become their official title!

Wenlock Edge Farm's beef, lamb, and chicken are carefully and locally-sourced for the best quality. Just as hams can be cooked and prepared to order, Wenlock Farm specialises in providing the best and highest quality cuts of these traditional staples. Supporting this, the delicatessen focuses on artisan and local producers who use traditional methods and local and seasonal produce to create small batches of goods where the emphasis is always on providing the best possible quality and taste experiences for the customer.

In an area renowned for its foodie focus, independent traders, and local produce, Wenlock Edge Farm's passion, experience, and commitment to the best quality and the highest standards clearly shines through. With two sites to choose from, including that rarest of beasts (a farm shop in the heart of the glorious county town of Shrewsbury), it's definitely the place to go to pig out!

Wenlock Edge Farm Shop

PORK, CHORIZO AND SWEET POTATO CASSEROLE

This dish contains Wenlock Edge Farm's own chorizo sausage. Made here on the farm it is a popular product in our charcuterie range. It is gluten-free, and if you choose to make this dish with gluten-free stock it would be perfect for anyone following a gluten-free diet.

Preparation time: 30 minutes | Cooking time: 1hour 30 minutes | Serves 4

Ingredients

2 tbsp olive oil

1 large onion, chopped

50g Wenlock Edge Farm chorizo, chopped

700g pork shoulder, diced

1 tbsp honey

2 cloves garlic, chopped

1 red chilli, chopped and seeds removed

1 x 400g tin of chopped tomatoes

500 ml chicken or veg. stock

2 or 3 sweet potatoes, peeled and cut into large chunks (keep the chunks large so they don't break up during cooking)

1 x 215g tin of kidney beans, rinsed

Salt and pepper (to taste)

Large handful of fresh coriander, chopped

Natural yogurt and crusty bread (to serve)

Method

Preheat the oven to 160°c, then, in a large casserole dish, heat 1tbsp of olive oil before adding in the chopped onion and chorizo. Gently fry these until they're softened and the oil is running from the chorizo. Remove these from the casserole dish using a slotted spoon, place in a bowl, and keep on one side. Adding the remaining tablespoon of olive oil to the casserole dish, heat and then use it to seal the diced pork shoulder. You may need to do this in two batches depending on the size of your dish.

Once all of the pork has been slightly browned, add in the onion and chorizo to the casserole dish and then blend in the chopped garlic and chilli. Stir well, making sure that all of the ingredients are evenly blended and then add the honey, chopped tomatoes, stock, plenty of salt and pepper and the sweet potatoes.

Raise this to the boil before replacing the lid on the casserole dish and placing it in the oven. After one hour, remove the casserole dish from the oven to add in the kidney beans. Stir these in well, and take the opportunity to check the seasoning, adding more if necessary before returning the casserole dish to the oven for a further half hour.

Serve topped with natural yogurt, fresh coriander and crusty bread to mop up the juices!

Viva la
REVOLUTION!

James Sherwin's Wild Shropshire ideas link the Shropshire countryside and the kitchen in inventive and dazzling ways...

Shropshire is the land of local produce. Not only does it produce some of the finest in the UK, but its foodies, restaurateurs, artisan producers and small-business owners flock to use it. But even in the county where the idea of local produce goes beyond faddish lip-service towards being a way of life, James Sherwin takes it further still. James is the founder of 'Wild Shropshire' – a Popup idea that looks to make the most of all of the countryside, not just the bits that grow behind fences.

"At Wild Shropshire we create food based on our environment in that environment," explains James. "That connection to locality is at the heart of what we do. It isn't just about what's been selling, but what people can buy, right here on their doorstep."

That end statement is a quotation from Guy Piccotto of the band Fugazi, but it underpins what James is doing. Regardless of what other restaurants and chefs are doing Wild Shropshire is all about taking responsibility. It's an ethical stance that informs everything from the source and choice of ingredients to the way they're prepared. Take the idea of seasonality. We all know that food tastes at its best when it's in season. That's why apples taste better in autumn and strawberries in summer

even though both are now available all the year 'round. But James goes beyond that, embedding his food in Shropshire's fertile landscape. The foodie term for it is 'foraging', but that implies picking up something that's been left behind, whereas what James does is use what's already there in abundance – Shropshire's open wild countryside. Take the birch ice-cream recipe, for example. It's a classic ice-cream recipe with a twist that invites the local environment into the kitchen and onto the plate. It's food that works closely with Shropshire's local farms, growers, and keepers to source products at the precise moment they reach their peak, sure. But it also pulls the wild landscape into the mix too.

The French call it 'terroir', the precise set of all geographical, environmental and farming factors that give any given crop in any given habit its distinctive character. They apply it to wine, but it could equally be applied to Wild Shropshire's ethos. It's more than a connection to Shropshire's rural character. It's a connection to the land's deep, rich history. As such, it offers an innovative and immersive approach to food, locality and seasonality that deserves to be on the end of your fork. So go on, take a walk on the wild side...

Wild Shropshire BIRCH

For the adventurous and those itching to extend their foraging and culinary repertoire, this dessert combines kitchen classics with wayfarer flavours

Preparation time: 12 hours | Cooking time: 45 minutes | Serves 4

Ingredients

For the birch cake:

700g flour

1 tsp baking powder

1 tsp bicarbonate of soda

½ tsp salt

340g birch syrup (For those who don't want to tap their own tree this can be bought online. Alternatively, substitute for the same amount of honey)

220g water

110g rapeseed oil

2 tsps cider vinegar

For the birch ice cream:

500ml double cream

750ml milk

280g sugar

2.5g salt

35g birch shavings

130g egg yolk

For the birch vinegar granita:

100g caster sugar

125ml water

300ml birch syrup (or substitute for the same amount of honey)

Cider vinegar

For the hazelnut meringue:

100g egg white

100g caster sugar

100g icing sugar

50g hazelnut, blitzed to a powder

For the garnish:

Apple marigold

Lemon verbena

Anise hyssop

Wood sorrel

Method

This recipe might appear complex, but by preparing the ice-cream and granita ahead of time it's actually quite simple.

For the birch ice cream

First, make the birch cream as follows. Preheat the oven to 70°c (or as low as it will go), put the double cream and birch shavings into a deep baking tray and mix thoroughly. Place in the oven and cook for 12 hours, leaving the door slightly open. After 12 hours add the milk, sugar and salt before sieving the cream mix to remove the wood and then put it to one side and allow it to cool. In a pan, add 600ml of the birch cream to the egg yolks and heat it until it reaches 80°c, and then cook at this temperature for 4 minutes. Pour mix into ice cream machine and run as per machine instructions.

For the birch vinegar granita

Put the birch syrup in a bowl, and add cider vinegar until the syrup tastes more sour than sweet. In a pan, combine the water and sugar before bringing to the boil and allowing the sugar to dissolve. Combine this mixture with the birch vinegar mixture. Allowing it to cool, check the resulting mixture for sourness. There should be a slight bite to it.

Once it has cooled sufficiently, place into a plastic tub and freeze. When ready to serve scrape with a fork to make fluffy

For the birch cake

Preheat oven to 180°c, oil a 22cm cake tin and then dust with flour. In a bowl, combine the flour, baking powder, bicarbonate of soda and salt evenly. In a separate bowl mix together the water, rapeseed oil, birch syrup, and cider vinegar before combining the wet and dry mixtures and blending them into a lump-free batter. Pour the batter into the cake tin and then cook for approx 25-30 minutes until the cake is set in the centre. Leave to cool for ten minutes before turning out onto a cooling rack

For the hazelnut meringue

Taking the egg whites already separated out from making the ice cream, use a kitchen mixer with the whisk attachment on to bring them to stiff peaks. Turning the whisk onto its slowest speed, slowly add in the caster sugar. Once the caster sugar has been added, slowly add the icing sugar, folding together until both are fully incorporated. Use some of the meringue to stick a sheet of greaseproof paper to a baking tray and then spread a thin layer of meringue mix over the top, using a large palette knife to smooth it out. Evenly sprinkle the hazelnut dust over the meringue. Bake in the oven at lowest possible temperature until dried out and crispy.

To serve

Cooling the serving bowls in a fridge for 15 minutes before serving, cut the cake into the desired size, place in a bowl, and add the other elements as you feel is right. At the last moment, add the granita and herbs and serve immediately.

The DIRECTORY

These great businesses have supported the making of this book; please support and enjoy them.

Albright Hussey Manor Hotel
Ellesmere Road
Shrewsbury SY4 3AF
Telephone: 01939 290571
Website: www.albrighthussey.co.uk
Long-established and with an illustrious history, Albright Hussey Manor Hotel offers beautifully elegant accommodation matched with a similar approach to food – using only the best local produce and overseen by chef Michel Nijsten the menu is based around the very best of Shropshire's seasonal produce.

Apley Farm Shop
Norton
Shropshire TF11 9EF
Telephone: 01952 581002
Website: www.apleyfarmshop.co.uk
A vibrant modern farm shop surrounded and supplied by one of England's finest historic estates, its food hall and welcoming café is crammed with wonderful local produce and it also offers a host of children's and arts and crafts activities.

Barkworths Seafoods
Stalls 16-17
Market Hall
Shrewsbury
Shropshire SY1 1HQ
Telephone: 01743 352138
Website: www.barkworths.co.uk
Located in Shrewsbury's famous market, Barkworths Seafoods and St. Pierre Seafood and Oyster Bar sells the highest quality fresh fish and seafood and wonderful freshly-made seafood, salad and soup respectively.

Battlefield 1403
Upper Battlefield
Shrewsbury SY4 3DB
Telephone: 01939 210905
Website: www.battlefield1403.co.uk
Exhibition centre on the site of the bloody Battle of Shrewsbury, with a farm shop, an artisan butcher and café Battlefield 1403 also offers a host of other activities for a day-out, including its falconry centre.

The Bear at Hodnet
Market Drayton
Shropshire TF9 3NH
Telephone: 01630 685214
Website: www.bearathodnett.co.uk
Historic coaching inn whose fantastic team offer a warm welcome, a fine selection of beers and wines alongside hearty pub fare, and accommodation in the charming village of Hodnet

Bennett-and-Dunn
Bridgnorth
Shropshire
Telephone: 07474 887453
Website: www.bennettanddunn.co.uk
Run by husband-and-wife team Richard and Tracey Bennett, the farm produces award-winning high-quality cold-pressed rapeseed oil whose creamy nutty flavour is increasingly garnering rave reviews from professional chefs and foodies alike.

Beth Heath Events
Bridge Farm
Buildwas Bank
Telford
TF8 7BN
Telephone: 01952 432175
Website: www.bethheathevents.co.uk
Specialising in drawing board to event delivery of everything from local to nationally-recognized events, Beth Heath Events has build an enviable national reputation as a consultancy, event management, marketing and press and promotions company.

The Boathouse
High Street
Clee Hill
Ludlow
SY8 3LZ
Telephone: 01743 231658
Website: www.boathouseshrewsbury. co.uk
One of Shrewsbury's favourite pubs, the Boathouse occupies a wonderful location next to the river Severn. Its bar and grill provides classic pub staples to a high standard with an inventive twist, reflecting the best of Shropshire's seasonal fare.

British Cassis
Whittern Farms
Lyonshall
Herefordshire
HR5 3JA
Telephone: 01544 340241
Website: www.whiterondrinks.co.uk
White Heron makes an award-winning blackcurrant liqueur drawn from founder Jo Hilditch's long-established Whittern Farm crop.

Café AleOli
Market Hall
Shrewsbury Market Hall
Claremont St
Shrewsbury SY1 1QG
Telephone: 01743 384253
Website: www.aleoli.co.uk
A friendly family business run by Frances O'Shea, AleOli brings the authentic flavours of Spanish tapas to Shrewsbury's ever-popular market.

The Castle Hotel
Bishop's Castle
Shropshire SY9 5BN
Telephone: 01588 638403
Website:
www.thecastlehotelbishopscastle.co.uk
An award-winning hotel and restaurant surrounded by some of Shropshire's most beautiful countryside, offering hearty flavoursome dishes, the best local beers, and a warm welcome to two and four-legged visitors alike.

The Coach House
Norbury
Bishop's Castle
Shropshire SY9 5DX
Telephone: 01588 650846
Website: www.coachhousenorbury.co.uk
Situated in the South Shropshire Hills Area of Outstanding Natural Beauty, the Coach House is a modern country inn offering bed and breakfast, dinner with the emphasis on local produce and drinks in a stylish relaxed space.

CSONS
8 Milk Street
Shrewsbury SY1 1SZ
Telephone: 01743 272709
Website: www.csons-shrewsbury.co.uk
Run and owned by four food-loving brothers, CSONS makes superb locally-sourced but globally inspired food in their beautifully atmospheric and inviting Shrewsbury restaurant.

The Chef's Locker
24 Chelmick Drive
Church Stretton
Shropshire SY6 7BP
Telephone: 01952 581002
Website: www.chefslocker.co.uk
Specialising in beautiful high-end Japanese kitchen knives and bespoke knife rolls and blocks, The Chef's Locker is a treasure trove of must-have kit for all foodies.

Darwin's Townhouse
37 St Julian's Friars
Shrewsbury
SY1 1XL
Telephone: 01743 34382
Website: www. darwinstownhouse.com
A three-storey townhouse just moments from the river Severn and Shrewsbury's town centre, Darwin's Townhouse offers a 20-bedroom boutique bed and breakfast experience.

The Haughmond
Pelham Rd
Shrewsbury
SY4 4TZ
Telephone: 01743 709918
Website: www.thehaughmond.co.uk
Offering award-winning fine dining and accommodation in a relaxed country atmosphere, the Haughmond offers superb formal and informal dining choices, specialising in the best of local produce and great service.

Havana Republic
18 Abbey Foregate
Shrewsbury
SY2 6AE
Tel: 01743 281744
Website: www.havanarepublic.co.uk
Bringing the vibrant party-led atmosphere of Cuba to Shrewsbury, with its rum, fantastic cocktails and great food Havana Republic serves Latino flavours infused with Caribbean spice and the hospitality of the Deep South.

Henry Tudor House
Barracks Passage
Shrewsbury SY1 1XA
Telephone: 01743 361666
Website: www.henrytudorhouse.com
Managed by the same team that run The New Inn at Baschurch, Henry Tudor House offers superb hospitality in its bar and restaurant with private dining available in one of Shrewsbury's oldest and most historic buildings.

The Hundred House
Norton (Ironbridge Gorge)
Telford
Shropshire TF11 9EE
Telephone: 01953 580240
Website: www.hundredhouse.co.uk
Run by the same family for over thirty years, this multi-award winning hotel and restaurant offers superb dining drawn from the local countryside, immaculate and atmospheric accommodation, and superb gardens in a beautiful part of Shropshire.

Kitchen Thyme
4 Darwin Court,
Oxon Business Park,
Shrewsbury, SY3 5AL
Telephone: 0785 5341 516
Website: www.kitchen-thyme.com
A Shropshire-based business run by Simply Good Food TV chef Sabrina Zeif, Kitchen Thyme runs bespoke culinary experiences, chef demonstrations and events, emphasizing global flavours, especially those of Cajun and Caribbean origin.

La Dolce Vita

35A Hill's Lane
Shrewsbury
SY1 1QU
Telephone: 01743 249126
Website: ladolcevitashrewsbury.co.uk
A long-established family-run
Italian restaurant whose inspired and
innovative menus, six-course gourmet
evenings, and excellent service in a
modern setting have garnered glowing
customer reviews.

Lane Cottage Produce

Richard and Amanda Sidgwick
Lane Cottage
Deerfold
Birtley
Bucknell
Herefordshire
SY7 0EF
Telephone: 01568 770720
Website:
www.lanecottageproduce.co.uk
A market garden founded by Richard and
Mandy Sidgwick, Lane Cottage grows
salad leaves and seasonal crops on organic
land, delivering fresh to local customers,
shops, and restaurants.

The Lion and Pheasant

49-50 Wyle Cop
Shrewsbury SY1 1XJ
Telephone: 01743 770345
Website: www.lionandpheasant.co.uk
An atmospheric townhouse hotel in the
heart of historic Shrewsbury, the Lion
and Pheasant offers delicious food on its à
la carte., lunch, and Sunday lunch menus
and boutiques-style accommodation.

The Loopy Shrew

15-17 Bellstone
Shrewsbury
Shropshire SY1 1HU
Telephone: 01743 366505
Website: www.loopyshrew.com
A family-run business owned and
managed by the same team that also
owns PorterHouse.SY1 and Darwin's
Townhouse, offering everything from
light bites to à la carte main courses,
a superb atmosphere, and boutique
accommodation.

The Market Hall,

Claremont Street,
Shrewsbury SY1 1QG
Telephone: 01743 351067
Website:
www.markethallshrewsbury.co.uk
A long established and much-loved
market in the heart of one of Britain's
most beautiful market towns, Shrewsbury
Market offers the best local produce,
artisanal food-makers, wonderful eateries,
and the full gamut of arts and handicrafts
among its stalls.

Maynard's Farm

Weston-under-Redcastle,
Shrewsbury
SY4 5LR
Telephone: 01948 840252
Website: www.maynardsfarm.co.uk
A farm shop dedicated to specialist pork
products that also offers lots of other
delicious local and British produce too,
alongside inspired catering for personal
and corporate functions.

Moli Tea House

Stall 12
The Market Hall
Claremont Street
Shrewsbury SY1 1QG
Telephone:
Website: www.markethallshrewsbury.
co.uk/cafe-restaurant-takeaway
Stall in Shrewsbury's acclaimed market
offering an authentic taste of China with
its hand-made dumplings and extensive
range of Sichuan-sourced loose leaf
Chinese tea.

Momo No Ki

19 Abbey Foregate
Shrewsbury
SY2 6AE
Telephone: 01743 281770
Website: www.momonoki.co.uk
The home of Ramen in Shrewsbury,
Momo No Ki serves delicious and
authentic Asian cuisine under the able
stewardship of Chris Burt, using the
freshest of ingredients from local suppliers.

Moyden's Cheese

Lockley Villa Farm
Wistanswick
Market Drayton
Shropshire TF9 2AY
Telephone: 01630 639796
Website: www.mrmoyden.com
Run by husband-and-wife team Martin
and Beth Moyden, Moyden's is highly
respected artisan cheese-making business
whose passion for quality and attention to
detail has resulted in an increasing list of
award-winning cheeses.

The New Inn at Baschurch

Church Road
Baschurch
Shrewsbury SY4 2EF
Telephone: 01939 260335
Website: www.newinnbaschurch.com
Managed by the same team that run
Shrewsbury's Henry Tudor House, The
New Inn at Baschurch brings all of the
best elements of a pub together: good food
and drink, served in atmospheric and
elegant surroundings.

Old Downton Lodge

Downton on the Rock
Ludlow
SY8 2HU
Telephone: 01568 771826
Website: www.olddowntonlodge.com
A multi-award winning lodge
offering sumptuous fine dining and
accommodation experiences amid the
picturesque Shropshire countryside.

Origins Restaurant

Shrewsbury College
130 London Rd
Shrewsbury
SY2 6PR
Telephone: 01743 342 611
Website:
www.shrewsbury.ac.uk/origins
Simultaneously a working restaurant and
centre of educational excellence, Origins
helps to train the next generation of chefs
and front-of-house staff while providing
an excellent classical and modern dining
experience for visiting customers.

The Peach Tree

18-21 Abbey Foregate
Shrewsbury
Shropshire
Telephone: 01743 355055
Website: www.thepeachtree.co.uk
Overseen by award-winning executive head chef Chris Burt, The Peach Tree serves handpicked ingredients drawn from Shropshire's farming communities to produce eclectic, inventive and flavoursome food.

PorterHouse.SY1

15 St Mary's St
Shrewsbury SY1 1EQ
Telephone: 01743 358870
Website: www.porterhousesy1.co.uk
Delivering big American flavours with the very best of British style and behaviour, PorterHouse. SY1 offers a fresh, funky venue for eating, drinking, or hanging out with boutique accommodation available.

Restaurant Severn

33 High Street
Ironbridge
Telford
TF8 7AG
Telephone: 01952 432233
Website: www.restaurantsevern.co.uk
An AA-recommended restaurant that combines French classical roots with the best of contemporary British cooking approaches for a superb dining experience.

The Riverside Inn

Aymestrey
Herefordshire
HR6 9ST
Telephone: 01568 708440
Website: www.riversideaymestrey.co.uk
Evocative inn in deep in the heart of the Shropshire countryside specialising in a 'seed-to-plate' ethos and atmospheric accommodation. Dog-friendly for walkers.

Smoked Shropshire

Pool Cottage
Poolhead
Wem
SY4 5QY
Telephone: 07969 998418
Email: smoked_shropshire@outlook.com
A street-food company with a burgeoning local reputation, specialising in low n' slow cooking that takes the best local produce and fires it through a world-food approach to produce fresh 100% homemade flavours.

Special Spuds

Gerrol and Alison Jalving
Jalving Potatoes UK Ltd
Meeson Hall Farm
Meeson
Nr Newport
Shropshire TF6 6PG
Telephone: 07976 621338
Website: www.specialspuds.co.uk
A third-generation family-run business, Jalving Potatoes specialise in cross-breeding potato varieties to develop and introduce more flavour, colour, and nutritional benefits into the great British spud.

Tanners Wines Ltd

26 Wyle Cop
Shrewsbury
Shropshire SY1 1XD
Telephone: 01743 234500
Website: www.tanners-wines.co.uk
Founded in 1842 and still family-run, Tanner's now encompasses seven branches as the UK's leading independent wine merchants. Priding itself on its traditional approach to customer service and high quality, Tanner's sells to quality minded hotels, restaurants, and outlets across the UK.

The Ugly Duckling

Long Lane,
Telford
TF6 6HA
Telephone: 01952 257979
Website: www.theuglyduckling.co.uk
A family-run welcoming bar and grill that varies and rotates its menus impressively to provide the perfect venue for get-togethers with family and friends or something a little more intimate.

Wenlock Edge Farm

Edge House
East Wall
Much Wenlock
Shropshire TF13 6DU
United Kingdom
East Wall Farm Shop: 01694 771893
Shrewsbury Shop: 01743 344464
Website: wenlockedgefarmshop.co.uk
A well-established and welcoming farm shop with sites in Shrewsbury and East Wall, Wenlock Edge Farm Shop offers award-winning pork and bacon alongside superb local and artisanal produce.

Wild Shropshire

Telephone: 07766 685076
Website: www.jamesinaspace.com
A Popup kitchen curated by James Sherwin, Wild Shropshire explores Shropshire's terroir, taking a seasonal foraging approach to food that results in innovative and connective menus based on location and participation.

The INDEX

C

Hay-baked Shropshire guinea fowl with carrot, barley and herbs 125
Smoked mutton with coconut dahl and mango salsa 133
Sticky toffee pudding with clotted cream and salted toffee sauce 137
Birch 145

Redcurrant jelly
Treacle-cured beef, chateau potatoes, braised shallots and chestnut mushrooms 121

Red onion
Salsa dressing 15
Pan-roasted sea bass fillet with warm salad of red onion, plum tomato and green beans 41
Sopresa AleOli 46
Agnolotti of smoked potato and onion 93

Red pepper
Sopresa AleOli 46

Red potato
Salmon and cod fishcake with Swedish beetroot salad 37

Red wine
Slowly braised lamb Henry 29
Breast of pigeon with Scotched quail's egg 77
Treacle-cured beef, chateau potatoes, braised shallots and chestnut mushrooms 121

Red wine vinegar
Treacle-cured beef, chateau potatoes, braised shallots and chestnut mushrooms 121

Rhubarb
Rhubarb and tonka bean parfait 61
Rhubarb and custard 109

Rice
Beijing dumplings with pork and cabbage 104

Rice vinegar
Beijing dumplings with pork and cabbage 104

Ricotta cheese
Sirloin of beef with glazed cheek parcel and ricotta gnocchi with wild garlic and chervil root 97

Roast ham
Proper eggs benedict 69

Rosemary
Slowly braised lamb Henry 29
Herb & garlic crusted rump of Welsh lamb, minted pea velouté & honey roasted root vegetables 51
Breast of pigeon with Scotched quail's egg 77
Roast lamb cutlet, braised belly and kidney croquette with roast onion purée 85
Hay-baked Shropshire guinea fowl with carrot, barley and herbs 125

S

Saffron
Countryside Caribbean bbq 89
Rhubarb and custard 109
Smoked mutton with coconut dahl and mango salsa 133

Sage
Slow roasted pork with fennel and lemon with sweet potato and coriander mash 103

Salad
Salsa dressing 15
Saladette of Shrewsbury fresh cheese 19
Salmon and cod fishcake with Swedish beetroot salad 37
Pan-roasted sea bass fillet with warm salad of red onion, plum tomato and green beans 41
Loopy's famous Scotch egg 71
Ultimate pulled pork burger 73
Slow roasted pork with fennel and lemon with sweet potato and coriander mash 103

Salmon
Salmon and cod fishcake with Swedish beetroot salad 37
Gin-cured salmon with celeriac remoulade and homemade blinis 43

Sausage
Loopy's famous Scotch egg 71
Breast of pigeon with Scotched quail's egg 77
Beijing dumplings with pork and cabbage 104
Duck cooked three ways with smoked pear 117
Pork, chorizo and sweet potato casserole 141

Sausage meat
Loopy's famous Scotch egg 71
Breast of pigeon with Scotched quail's egg 77

Sea bass
Pan-roasted sea bass fillet with warm salad of red onion, plum tomato and green beans 41

Self-raising flour
Chocolate & orange brownie tray bake & flower pots 53
Sticky toffee pudding with clotted cream and salted toffee sauce 137

Sesame oil
Beijing dumplings with pork and cabbage 104

Shallot
Breast of pigeon with Scotched quail's egg 77
Agnolotti of smoked potato and onion 93
Sirloin of beef with glazed cheek parcel and ricotta gnocchi with wild garlic and chervil root 97
Duck cooked three ways with smoked pear 117

Shaoxing wine
Beijing dumplings with pork and cabbage 104

Sichuan pepper
Beijing dumplings with pork and cabbage 104

Sirloin
Sirloin of beef with glazed cheek parcel and ricotta gnocchi with wild garlic and chervil root 97

Smoked bacon
Slowly braised lamb Henry 29

Smoked newport
Moyden's cheese four ways 23

Smoked paprika
Purple sprouting broccoli with polenta, muhamarra, poached egg and Parmesan 65
Ultimate pulled pork burger 73
Countryside Caribbean bbq 89

Snack
Loopy's famous Scotch egg 71

Soy sauce
Chilli and miso buttered roasted duck noodle soup 56
Countryside Caribbean bbq 89
Beijing dumplings with pork and cabbage 104

Spinach
Duck cooked three ways with smoked pear 117

Spring onion
Countryside Caribbean bbq 89

Squash
Treacle-cured beef, chateau potatoes, braised shallots and chestnut mushrooms 121

Star anise
Breast of pigeon with Scotched quail's egg 77
Agnolotti of smoked potato and onion 93

Steak
Salsa dressing 15

Sugar
Pan-roasted sea bass fillet with warm salad of red onion, plum tomato and green beans 41
Gin-cured salmon with celeriac remoulade and homemade blinis 43
Chocolate & orange brownie tray bake & flower pots 53
Rhubarb and tonka bean parfait 61
Ultimate pulled pork burger 73
Countryside Caribbean bbq 89
Agnolotti of smoked potato and onion 93
Sweet pastry with lemon curd and Italian meringue 99
Beijing dumplings with pork and cabbage 104
Rhubarb and custard 109
Pork with onion, mushroom and miso 113
Treacle-cured beef, chateau potatoes, braised shallots and chestnut mushrooms 121
Sticky toffee pudding with clotted cream and salted toffee sauce 137
Birch 145

Swede
Herb & garlic crusted rump of Welsh lamb, minted pea velouté & honey roasted root vegetables 51

Sweet potato
Slow roasted pork with fennel and lemon with sweet potato and coriander mash 103

Other titles in the 'Get Stuck In' series

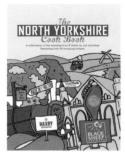

The North Yorkshire Cook Book
features Andrew Pern, Visit
York, Made in Malton, Black
Sheep Brewery and lots more.
978-1-910863-12-1

The Birmingham Cook Book
features Glynn Purnell, The
Smoke Haus, Loaf Bakery,
Simpsons and lots more.
978-1-910863-10-7

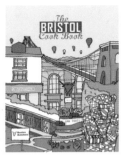

The Bristol Cook Book
features Dean Edwards, Lido,
Clifton Sausage, The Ox, and
wines from Corks of Cotham
plus lots more.
978-1-910863-14-5

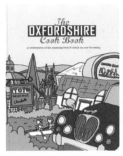

The Oxfordshire Cook Book
features Mike North of The
Nut Tree Inn, Sudbury House,
Jacobs Inn, The Muddy Duck
and lots more.
978-1-910863-08-4

The Lancashire Cook Book
features Andrew Nutter of
Nutters Restaurant, Bertram's,
The Blue Mallard and lots
more.
978-1-910863-09-1

The Liverpool Cook Book
features Burnt Truffle, The
Art School, Fraiche, Villaggio
Cucina and many more.
978-1-910863-15-2

**The Sheffield Cook Book
- Second Helpings**
features Jameson's Tea Rooms,
Craft & Dough, The Wortley
Arms, The Holt, Grind Café
and lots more.
978-1-910863-16-9

The Leeds Cook Book
features The Boxtree,
Crafthouse, Stockdales of
Yorkshire and lots more.
978-1-910863-18-3

The Cotswolds Cook Book
features David Everitt-
Matthias of Champignon
Sauvage, Prithvi, Chef's Dozen
and lots more.
978-0-9928981-9-9

The Suffolk Cook Book
features Jimmy Doherty of
Jimmy's Farm, Gressingham
Duck and lots more.
978-1-910863-02-2

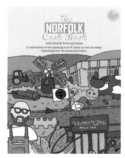

The Norfolk Cook Book
features Richard Bainbridge,
Morston Hall, The Duck Inn
and lots more.
978-1-910863-01-5

The Lincolnshire Cook Book
features Colin McGurran of
Winteringham Fields,
TV chef Rachel Green,
San Pietro and lots more.
978-1-910863-05-3

The Newcastle Cook Book
features David Coulson
of Peace & Loaf, Bealim
House, Grainger Market,
Quilliam Brothers and lots
more.
978-1-910863-04-6

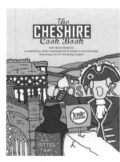

The Cheshire Cook Book
features Simon Radley of
The Chester Grosvenor, The
Chef's Table, Great North
Pie Co., Harthill Cookery
School and lots more.
978-1-910863-07-7

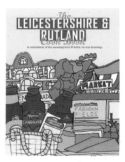

**The Leicestershire & Rutland
Cook Book** features Tim Hart
of Hambleton Hall, John's
House, Farndon Fields,
Leicester Market, Walter
Smith and lots more.
978-0-9928981-8-2

*All books in this series are available from Waterstones,
Amazon and independent bookshops.*

FIND OUT MORE ABOUT US AT WWW.MEZEPUBLISHING.CO.UK